TO THE PERSON
WHO TOOK THE SAW IN HAND AND RESOLVED TO CUT THE FENCE
AND NOT THE FLOWERING TREE.

WE STARED AT THE caretaker's fence in amazement. We don't have a fence like that in Russia yet. Who knows how long it will take? It took over ten years just to discover that such a thing existed. Do you understand that a fence like that can only come to be very slowly? It is possible that it's taken most of America's history. It obviously represents the work of someone who understands *life*. For a person to take a saw and cut a hole in his fence, he must know more about life than the workings of a market economy. The caretaker's work means more to us than anything we've seen so far of democracy.

After ten years we have not yet seen democracy, or a stable economy, or happier lives—despite the fact that we now have plenty of MacDonalds, and corporate business plans, and "secondhand stores" (something we never had before). These weren't worth waiting seventy years for. The caretaker's fence on the other hand—no one can say that that is not right! There will always be something to be said for doing those things that "reason" screams make absolutely no difference. For they are the things, like the hole in the fence, *that give life*.

NIKOLAI ARJANNIKOV
Moscow, Russia

Editor
Margaret Robinson Millar

Make a hole in the fence

photograph by
Valerie Schurer Christle

ARJANNIKOV AND FERBER

ANDOVER GREEN BOOK PUBLISHERS
ALTON NH

Make a hole in the fence

Nikolai Mikailovich Arjannikov and Jeannie Ferber
Copyright © 2002 Andover Green Book Publishers
All rights reserved. First Printing

BOOKS@WORLDPATH.NET

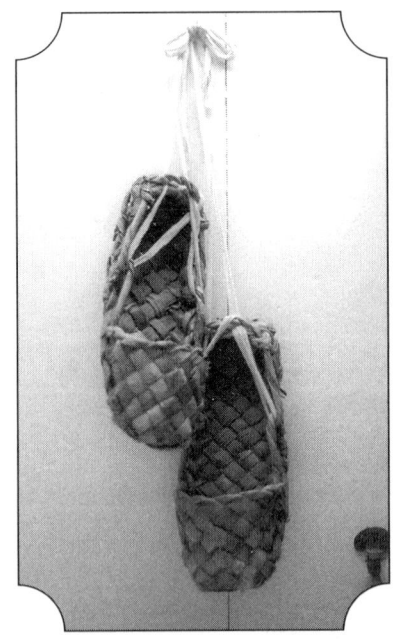

Printed by
Accura Printing Company
So. Barre, Vermont

C

PART I
Through the hole in the fence
1

PART II
Gently come, Gently go
39

AFTERWORD
A book that became a library
82

Moskva
DEPART 9:00 AM

ONE LANE ROADS MOST OF THE WAY ✥ AVERAGE SPEED 50 MPH.

Vladimir

Nizhni Novgorod
DUSK FALLS
5:00 PM

Volga River

THE JOURNEYS

1st journey: Moskva to Vetoshkino

750 MILES ✝ 22 HOURS

2nd journey: Vetoshkino to Pervouralsk

700 MILES ✝ 18 HOURS

3rd journey: Pervouralsk to Moskva

1800 MILES ✝ 30 HOURS

WITH EACH JOURNEY A NEW SMALL LIBRARY IS OPENED IN

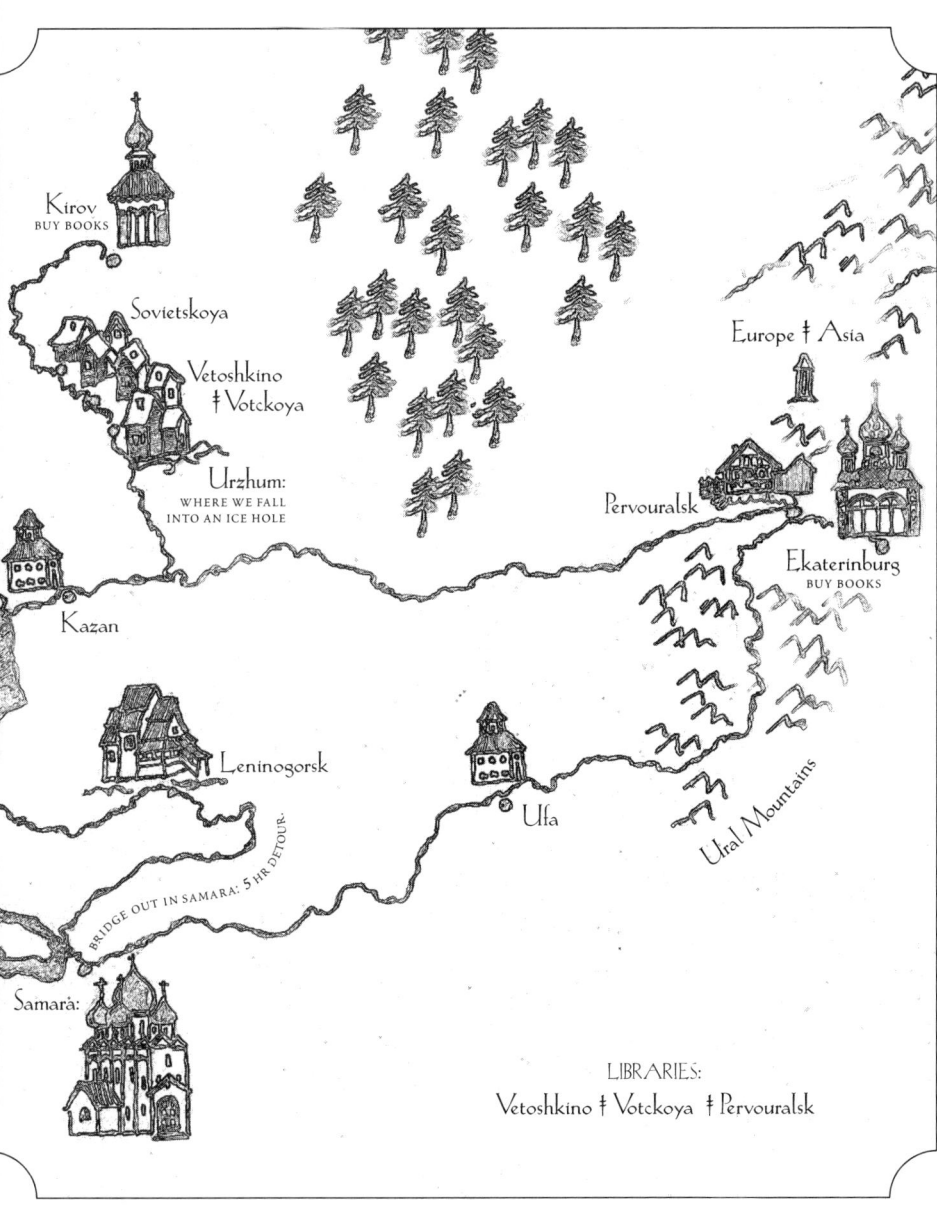

SOME VILLAGE, AND A FENCE IS LEFT WITH A HOLE IN IT.

VETOSHKINO RUSSIA

PART I
THROUGH THE HOLE IN THE FENCE

Vetoshkino, Russia
March 20, 2002

It was the first day of spring according to the calendar, but still the middle of winter in Russia. Even now it is hard to believe how we ever made it to Vetoshkino ∾ let alone think what has happened since. We were there, in part, to open a library in the school. It had been Nikolai's job to get us there, and mine to record the tale. The village had been settled in the mid-1800s and was little changed. I was, they said, the first American ever to set foot there. I was far from my New England home ∾ though not merely because I had traveled nearly 8000 miles to get there. I had gone back in time. It is a rare event in real life, despite the fact that anything is possible in Russia. There my name was Zhenne, the Russian of Jeannie. Let it only be added, that to Nikolai Mikhailovich the village was neither remote nor obscure. It was Russia. All along he understood what could happen there. Even there.

We were so exhausted by the time we arrived, that I don't remember falling asleep, only awakening hours later on a small cot draped with a heavy blue and white tapestry coverlet whose lead weight I couldn't shake off in my hot, half-awake state. As my eyes began to adjust to the morning light, the room began very pleasantly to describe itself to me: my cot occupied a small corner and stood only two feet from the backside of a large Russian wood burning stove.

My eyes went up to a small window above my head, filled with what seemed to be noonday light. The bright rays took my gaze to the opposite wall—no more than a few feet from the end of the bed. They illuminated a lovely wooden shelf (carved, no doubt, by a master), upon which lay someone's hat. Beneath the shelf were eight evenly spaced pegs, two of which had coats on them. Two pairs of muddy boots, it appeared, had been hastily left next to the large worn wooden door. As far as I could tell, it was the only door into the room, though I had no recollection of coming through it.

The massive wood burning stove—easily five feet in length at its base and three feet where it met the ceiling—kept me from seeing more of the room. There was something about the stove, apart from either its size, the crackle of the fire, or its soft whitewashed sides, that held my gaze to it transfixed. I had thought them to exist only in fancifully written fairy tales, and not in a place where you could actually awake. Yet the coats hanging there on their wooden pegs, and the boots cast carelessly in a pile, were clearly mine and Nikolai's.

Somewhere outside a rooster began to crow and then somewhat nearer a man could be heard calling to his wife. *Zdeec, ceno`valye!* "I'm here, in the hayloft!" It was from somewhere on the other side of the divided room, however, that a deep familiar voice called out, *"Are you awake?"*

Immediately, it all came back: the trip from Boston to Moscow, where I was, why I was here, and the reason for the muddy boots.

It was already the third week in March when Nikolai and I left Moscow by car and set out for Vetoshkino where he had arranged for us to launch our second library project. The "us" were people literally from all over the world who, learning of our efforts to open small libraries in villages throughout Russia, had helped in countless ways to make that possible. The thought of it brought no end of joy to Nikolai. Every time he thought of it he would say, "Jeannie! A log will never burn alone. But when there are many . . . *what warmth and light!*"

Our journey was to take us past countless villages all of which, like Vetoshkino, were unnamed on any map. Choosing where to go was a matter of where your Uncle Vanya or Aunt Olga lived. Vetoshkino is where Nikolai's great aunt and cousins live and, for no more complex reason than that, Vetoshkino was where we would be working. Nikolai's cousin, Tatyana, had made all the necessary arrangements with the tall lanky director of Vetoshkino Middle School, Sergei Evgenevich, who bowed politely whenever he met anyone, and held both your hands in his when he said good-bye. It was also Tatyana who had been trying to find her husband Mikhail that morning in the barn. The barn, courtyard, guest room, and house are all linked together very cleverly. It is the main house, however, that is the clasp holding it all together.

~ THE RESHETHIKOV HOME ~

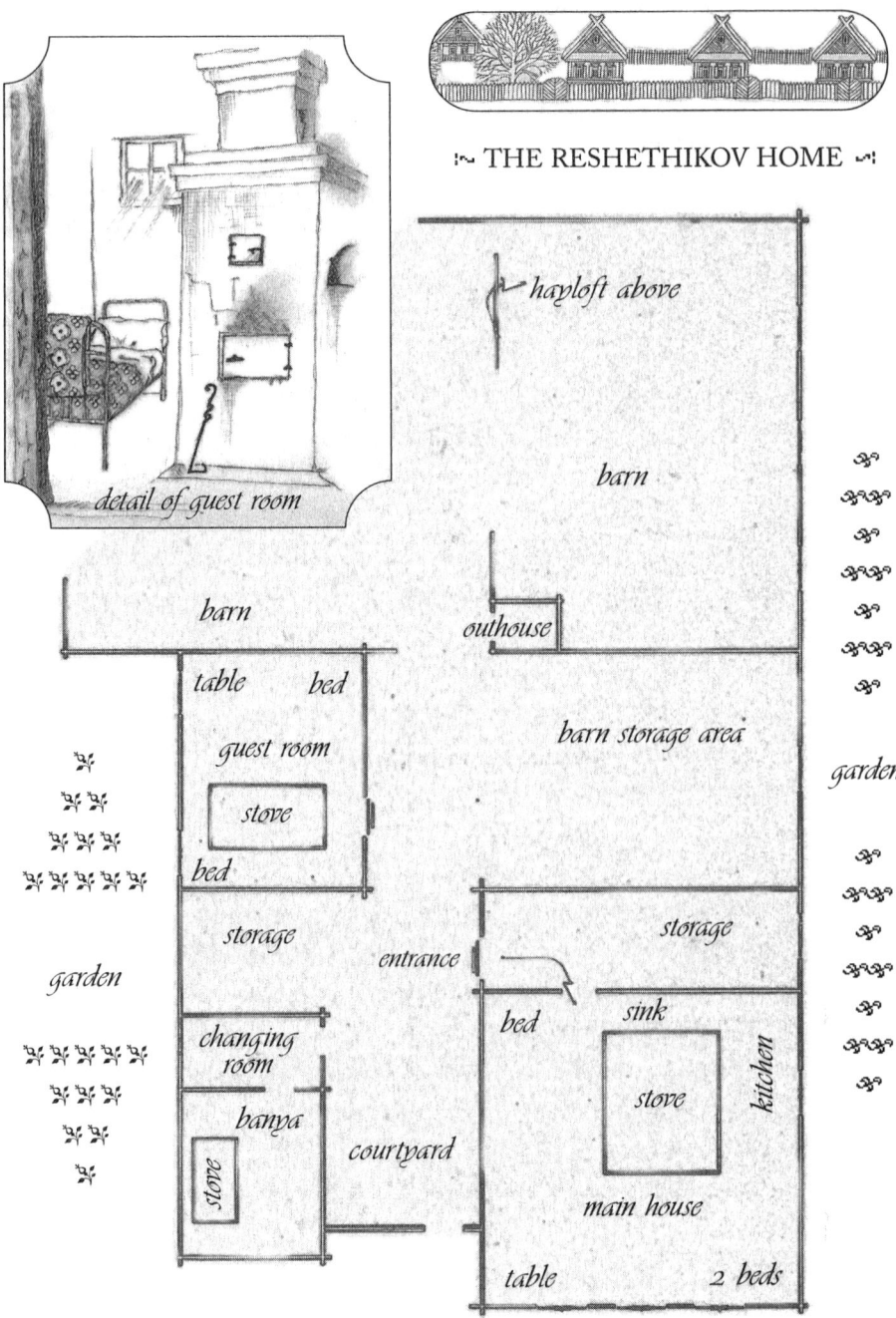

The main house is one large cozy room. In the area to the left of the entry is a porcelain wash basin with a small tin water tank hanging above it. A spout pulls down and lets spurts of water out. Next to the wash basin is a small kitchen. Beyond that, in the next corner, are two faded cotton curtains, behind which are two small cots, one for *Babushka* (grandmother) Natasha and the other for young Sasha. The third corner is where the table sits, and where we eat and drink tea, and talk endlessly. The fourth corner, to the right of the entry, is curtained off by two large oriental rugs and is where Tatyana and Mikhail and three of their five cats fall asleep at night. The stove is the center of the house, and the center of life. *Babushka* pulls out of its deep ovens golden loaves of freshly made bread and meat-filled *piroshki*, while Sasha keeps it filled with offerings from oak and silver birch trees. On the coldest nights Mikhail climbs atop it to sleep. But I've strayed from my explanation of the reason for the muddy boots.

I had been designated as the navigator of our trip. I said nothing, simply because my Russian wasn't adequate and the morning had already gotten off to a rocky start—leaving us stuck in early morning Moscow traffic breathing clouds of car exhaust and staring at hard, black piles that once had been snow. Ahead of us lay a journey of some 750 miles over the still snowbound, isolated roads of winter Russia, and before me a map which, it appeared, bore none of the roads over which we needed to travel. The miniscule Cyrillic letters jostled and jumped on the page as our car pounded over the "highway". Over and over again Nikolai repeated our route, saying the names of the cities most likely to be on the map, at times spelling them out slowly, letter by letter. Our journey would take us beyond Vladimir, Nizhni Novgorod, Kazan and Malmizh —and finally, beyond all semblance of the 21st century. The fact that the map listed none of the villages in, or around, our destination was apparently an inconsequential detail—or *poostyak*—as Nikolai liked to say. He had been there once before, he calmly assured me, as a boy.

Only toward dusk did grey factory towns give way to slumbering villages and snow that was soft and white and clean. It was about five o'clock when we finally stopped at a roadside café to get something hot to eat. The proprietor was a round-faced woman with a gentle smile and kindly eyes who soon brought out two steaming bowls of borsch and fresh bread, followed by a plate of *pelmini* —a spicy meat-filled pasta dish. In the background a cassette was playing. The song, simply called "Mama," was beautiful, comforting—and typically Russian.

I began musing silently over our long day. How many hours, I wondered, did we have left? At one point I had tried to figure out how many kilometers we could travel in an hour. Not long before, a road sign had said that Kazan was still 335 kilometers away. Less than a minute later another claimed that it was actually 315. When the next sign said 355 kilometers, I stopped reading them.

In the midst of this musing, I hadn't been aware that Nikolai had gotten up to pay the bill. It was only when the music suddenly stopped that the silence brought me back to the table and my still unfinished plate of *pelmini*. Nikolai came back to the table with an apologetic look on his face that said we needed to keep going . . . and in his hand the cassette that had just been playing. He had mentioned to the proprietor how much I loved it.

The villages got fewer and farther between, and it was much longer now between times when we'd pass someone on the road. The sun had made its silent journey across the sky, pulling us farther and farther along, carrying us from one time zone to another—and from one world to another. As soon as the sun set, the temperature fell dramatically and people took shelter in the warmth of their homes. Only an occasional jack rabbit would dart across the road, or an owl swoop through the dim beam of our headlights.

It was 2:00 in the morning, seventeen hours after we left Moscow, when we finally reached Urzhum, the last town of any size—and only twenty-five miles from our destination. Here we came upon a lone man walking his dog, the heads of both bent down against the wind and the cold. We stopped the man to ask about the condition of the road. His breath hung in the air and froze as he spoke. His dog pawed at clumps of ice dangling from the matted fur on either side of his nose. Of the two roads open, the man advised, the one to the right was the more likely to be passable.

We drove on past the last few houses but, on an intuition, Nikolai stopped at the very last house and knocked gently on the lower right pane of the front window. The curtain pulled back showing the weary face of a man who nodded understandingly. The drape fell limply back into place and then, moments later, the man appeared from behind the courtyard door. He, too, confirmed that the road to the right was the better chance.

We started out again peering reluctantly ahead as the road grew more and more impassable: a sea of frozen ice heaved up here—or with gaping holes there. We inched along, straddling huge ruts, and holding our breath every time the ground groaned and cracked beneath us. Finally, the ground simply gave way and the road disappeared before our eyes. Half the car lay engulfed in an ice hole. Every attempt to get out proved futile and only dug us in deeper. There was no alternative but for me to wait in the car while Nikolai went for help.

My main thought was to keep warm. I drew my hood over the hat I was already wearing and began running my hand across the seat feeling for my mittens. At last, my fingers felt a lumpy object beneath them. I heard myself gasp.... It wasn't my mittens. It was Nikolai's hat. The temperature was below zero and Nikolai is totally bald.

At that point I had no way of knowing that, as Nikolai walked through the night, the man to whom he last spoke had left his home to find us. Together the two of them walked thirty minutes to the home of a man with a large truck. It was nearly 3:30 in the morning when the bright headlights broke through the darkness where I watched. Nikolai emerged from the cab and gratefully put on the knitted cap still clutched in my hand. He was noticeably chilled—even before the nearly hour of numbing work it took to get us out.

I clambered over the chunks of ground strewn across the road, calling out to the men, thanking them over and over again. At last, one of them motioned me to be still. "Woman, why are you thanking us as if we just saved your life? Nothing awful ever happens! It's all just an adventure!" And with that, our unknown helpers disappeared into the stillness of the night.

The sun had begun to spill its first soft light over the edge of another day when we turned into Vetoshkino— twenty-two hours after we had left Moscow. Tatyana and Mikhail, already up since 4:00 a.m., greeted us anxiously, pulling off our boots, and wrapping us in warm blankets and soft *valenki* (tall, felt boots). Tatyana quickly filled the kitchen table with hot food. For Nikolai there was a shot of vodka—and, for me, hot milk baked in the deep upper oven of the stove, magically caramelizing the cream on the top. It was then that I first fell into the little cot, overcome by a sleep as deep as all the enchantments that befall innocent characters in Russian fairy tales.

"Are you awake?" Nikolai repeated in a voice that was half asleep. "It seems that we are still living and I am very hungry!" I could hear the floor boards creaking on his side of the room. He was dressing. As one who had lived all his life in such circumstances, he knew just what to do. I asked him once (knowing that he had shared a room with his grandmother when he was growing up) if he had ever seen her unclothed. Even as I asked I apologized—saying it was just one of those things Americans couldn't imagine. "Of course not!" he had answered, shocked by the question. "She was a woman!"

Now fully clothed, Nikolai quickly crossed the room and exited. I was left alone to dress ... and to explore the other side of the stove with its many little cast iron doors —the best of which was a large arched one in the center.

I was staring into this when Tatyana came to let me know that *obeyed*, or dinner, was ready. Had I ever seen such a stove, she asked? I answered by shaking my head, "No." But how did I prepare dinner?

In Russia, dinner always begins with soup and fresh bread. This being a farm, there are always bowls of thick homemade sour cream and plates filled with huge chunks of newly made butter. The meat, fish, vegetables, mushrooms, and pickles had all been put up in the fall. With a huge smile, Mikhail produced a bar of chocolate.

We ate quickly as the children of Vetoshkino Middle School were awaiting us. Donning our coats and hats and boots, we stepped out into the sunshine along a road laden with fresh snow and centuries of history, past scenes that Tolstoy had written about endlessly.

Another normal day had begun in Russia. . . .

"Shakespeare, please."

As far as we knew, none of the children had ever owned

books of their own. The school did have a small existing library of maybe a dozen bookshelves. The books clearly had been beautiful in their day, but the newest of them was from the early 1950s, and this was now 2002. The geography book I held in my hands was filled with faded continents and names of countries that no longer existed.

The grey cement block school building built in 1948 stood in sharp contrast to the village's more gentle homes

—and abruptly brought to mind another era with all its complex history. The thoughts were fleeting, however, as we stepped through the heavy wooden front door and into the warmth of the welcome that awaited us.

Arrangements were made for us to visit two different classes followed by a session with the teachers. An assistant scurried from the office to notify them of our arrival. A beautiful young boy, with delicate features and soft brown hair, cut in a perfect bowl around his head, peered through the door to say that his class was eager to welcome us. It was only then—as means of an embarrassed explanation for the child's innocent, wide-eyed stare—that an assistant hastily explained that an American had never come to the village before.

We were led down the one main hall whose tall ceiling absconded with most of the pale yellow light coming from three light bulbs dangling precariously from their electrical cords. The upper half of the walls was white, and the lower a rich, and typically Russian, shade of deep blue-green. A heavy wooden door to the classroom was swung open—bringing the students leaping to attention. They stood rod straight next to their desks, though their necks were noticeably straining to the left to get a better look at "the visitors". After being led to a raised platform, the teacher invited us to sit down. In perfect unison the students intoned the formal Russian greeting, and only then returned to their seats, their huge eyes peering at us in silent, intense anticipation of what was to come.

Nikolai's words were running through my head, "A child's first impression is the strongest and most lasting. When they see you, they will not be seeing an individual. They will think of you as 'America'."

What were they thinking? They were so solemn and silent. Were they anxious? After all, they were still children. Did they notice my staring at their unadorned simple clothes? At the girls' beautiful braided hair, or at the boys' wonderful bowl shaped haircuts? At the noticeable purity of their faces? At the innocence our world had not managed to steal from them? It was their innocence that was so startling. Here, in this far-off Russian village, it was clear and unmistakable that the West had been horribly tricked out of its innocence.

The children sat two to a desk, the desks being wooden and painted the same shade of deep blue-green. Their teacher's introduction was done and now they were waiting anxiously to see what I was going to say. I knew more than anything else—they wondered what I was thinking about them. I had planned to start by sharing my warm impressions of Russia. Yet, suddenly, I realized that that was not enough. Only if I could get these understandably shy children to open up with me would there be any hope of some *feeling* between us. But how to do that?

Children everywhere love to be helpful, an inner voice prompted. And so I heard myself saying that I was only learning Russian, and if I made a mistake (they giggled and so I knew I just had) would they help me? It worked. A hand went up. I should have said *osheebkoo*, instead of *osheebka*, for the word "mistake". (It was the object and not the subject of the sentence, a girl in the front politely explained—and thus was in the accusative case!)

Then she asked how I had learned Russian? In part, I said, by listening to Russian music. I played it cooking dinner, cleaning the house, and driving in the car. In the summer, I made a special point of playing it loudly.... I gestured and they understood that I didn't know how to say "with all the car windows rolled down". A boy in the back provided the needed phrase and then asked if I could read a book in Russian yet?

"Only *Winnie-the-Pooh*," I said.

They laughed.

With his beaming eyes, Nikolai was telling me that I should keep going. What was America *really* like, they wanted to know? Could our countries be friends?

In Nikolai's mind these minutes were as important as the library work itself. While the primary work was, of course, to bring a library alive, the leaving behind of even a thousand books could not of itself meet the great need to heal distrust and fear—as well as deeply held misconceptions. And none was deeper than the image of "rich soulless Americans".

Now Nikolai took over. He had moved his chair next to mine but was hardly sitting in it. He spoke decisively—everywhere we went making the same three points that, as simply and swiftly as turning a combination lock, spun first this way, then that . . . and then, "click," a little door inside the heart would open. If his words never ceased to surprise me, they got people nodding understandingly:

◈ "Children, we only have a very short time together. Please listen carefully! You know we are here to buy new books for your library, but that is not the most important thing. The most important thing is not *what* you do, but *how* you do it. Jeannie has come from America not simply with money—but with the help of many people who have worked hard to enable us to do this. We are here only because of their hard work and caring.

◈ "Each morning Jeannie reads the Bible and prays. [Later Nikolai explained that faith practiced privately is considered more honest and genuine.]

❧ "Our real hope is that people of all countries will one day come to respect and understand one another."

At last, Nikolai told the children the final reason for our being there. "All the people who helped us get here," he began, "wanted you each to have a book of your own. We need to have you tell us the book you want."

Not one child spoke. We waited. . . .

Their distraught faces made plain what was happening: had they misunderstood? What were they supposed to do? Were they really supposed to speak up—or were their teachers going to answer for them? If you could own one book of your own, what would you choose? They cast quick glances at their seat partners and then looked down. They gripped their pencils in both hands. Their teachers waited anxiously. The minutes dragged on painfully.

Now Nikolai was up and out of his chair trying to reassure them that they *were* supposed to answer freely. He walked back and forth in front of them but, having been raised in such a school, could not bring himself to go as far as to walk down the aisles among them. Remaining in front, he nonetheless spoke encouragingly: now trying to guess what was going through their heads, now trying to find one brave enough to begin. "You are free to decide what you want! We expect you to speak up. We do not want you to say what you think we want to hear, or what you think your teachers want to hear! You are to tell us what you *really* want. *Dyevushka*, [young girl] begin!"

The large-eyed, blond haired girl in the front left row

barely spoke, shyly asking for an encyclopedia of biology and then, as if she'd lose her courage, her seat mate quickly asked for an encyclopedia of geology.* Then came the boy who had been chosen to go to the office and escort us to his class. His delicate features made him look far too young to be a part of a high school class. "Could I have a book of Shakespeare, please?" That brought a hand from the back of the room, "Please, that is what I want also!" Soon, their voices began to ring out confidently and happily. One wanted Hemingway. (The Russian alphabet has no letter **H** and so it came out *Gemingway*). Another asked for Conan Doyle and then another for Dumas. As the names rolled off their tongues I sat amazed: Walter Scott, Mark Twain and, of course, all the names that had made Russian literature great, Tolstoy, Pushkin, Chekhov, Lermontov, and on and on.

All the while Tatyana and the teachers took copious notes making sure not a single request was missed. Too soon the bell rang and it was time to say good-bye. Two years of work was over. As the students filed out, glancing back over their shoulders and smiling, I thought of all the incredible people who had worked so hard to help us. Where were they? Why weren't they here to see the children's faces and share their joy? "Nikolai," I whispered. "How can we share this?" There wasn't time to answer, as a class of eleventh graders was filing in.

That class went much like the first, with it, too, being over far too soon. It was then time to meet the staff and teachers. One of them approached us saying, before we

*There are beautiful single volume encyclopedias as well as multiple volumes.

began there was to be a surprise. Another teacher was already putting a tape into a cassette player—the sight of which jolted me briefly back into the 21st century—but only momentarily. A very beautiful dark haired girl named Lena was approaching us. Her hair was pulled back and tied with a ribbon. She smiled eagerly. She would like to sing for us. I caught sight of Nikolai's eyes. It was not just the beauty of the song. *It was that we were hearing it.* His eyes said we had "broken through".

Then another teacher rose to say that they would like to sing a few songs for us. Igor Mikhailovich, a very rural looking man with rosy cheeks and a wisp of hair that fell pleasantly out of control on his forehead, walked up to the front of the room carrying a pale green accordion. He bowed slightly, thanked us for coming, and then threw back his head and began to play and sing.

When he finished, the room burst into applause yet he was already on to the next song. The teachers recognized it and picked up the melody in perfect unison. The room swayed. Their hands danced above their heads while their feet kept up the beat on the well-worn wooden floor. No longer able to contain himself, Nikolai left my side to join the teachers. He sat down at an empty desk grabbing the sides of it, rocking happily back and forth until the last of their songs finally drew to a close. Then Nikolai rejoined me, saying we must now share something with them. He had taught me one verse of a song as old as Russia itself. "*Toe nay veeter . . .*" we began. "It is not the wind that is making the branches tremble. . ."

This old loved Russian custom of singing for people had taken a long time to get used to, until one day Nikolai simply explained that you sing for others for the very same reason you sing for yourself when you're alone.

Nikolai and I were then invited back to the director's office. Just as we got to the door, it swung open of its own accord followed by a stout little woman wearing a faded apron and a glowing smile, and carrying an empty tray in her hand. She bowed politely and stared at us with all the eagerness and joy of one who had done her best. There, laid out on Sergei Evgenevich's long conference desk, was a feast that seemed impossible for this one little woman to have prepared all by herself. There were two or three boards filled with freshly made bread, three platters of fruits and salads (where had these come from in midwinter?), six large bowls of hot, steaming borsch, and a huge plate of *pelmini* in the center. A bottle of wine and another of vodka stood at the director's place, as well as several bottles of fruit juices, more costly than the alcohol. Contrary to most everyone's predictions, no one ever took objection to my not drinking alcohol. Occasionally, when Nikolai explained it was religiously based, it would result in a thoughtful discussion of the things of God—though this was a subject I never initiated.

At last a cake was produced and a box of chocolates, followed by incredibly touching handmade gifts from the children as well as the teachers. Their greatest gift, however, remained their way of life. More than once, I tried to tell the children just how much their lives had touched me. Sadly, through my broken Russian, it was impossible for them to conceive that I was *really* saying a small Russian village had something to teach Americans.

An American in the village

At home, we talked well into the night, making plans for our trip to Kirov to buy books. Mikhail, up at four every morning, finally climbed atop the stove to sleep, knowing all that would fall to him the next day. Were he not Russian, Mikhail would make a perfect Dicken's character. He is a lithe man of incredible strength, with a long, sinewy face, and angular nose. His hair is thin and oily,

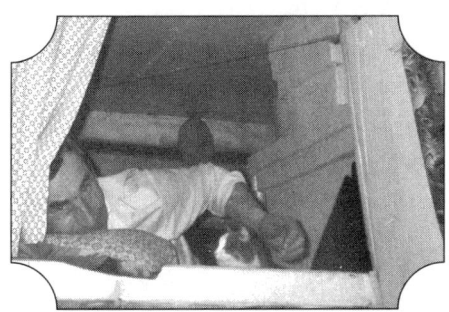

his cheeks permanently red, and his beard coarse, black, and stubbly. He works tirelessly, yet his eyes shine with the light of one who lives with utter, inner contentment. His favorite cat had followed him up the ladder to sleep beside him.

Babushka, however, was still wide awake—and utterly engrossed in the conversation. Only when her hands lay in her lap did they look thick and old, but her face *never*. All it took was a lump of dough or spinning wool and her hands were once again a child's.

Babushka's face is always wrapped in a head scarf, presenting a stereotype of simplicity that falls far short of her remarkable life and sharp mind. Born into tsarist Russia, she had lived to see the rise and fall of communism, space travel, the computer revolution, and the dawn of democracy. As definite on her views of communism's inevitable doom as she was on the need for democracy—she sat up late into the night listening intently to our discussions. I might be the first American she'd ever met, yet that did *not* mean she wasn't keenly aware of her world. Amazingly foresighted, she would say that although the transition was *hard*, life was bound to improve under democracy.

For the first two days I had been very uncomfortable about being waited on, not only by Tatyana, but *Babushka* especially. Neither would sit down until everyone else had been served. *Babushka* even waited until we had finished, fussing in the kitchen or scurrying between rooms refilling bowls of food until she was satisfied that everyone had been well fed. Nikolai had told me ahead of time that Tatyana alone would decide when I was allowed in the kitchen. But until then, it was a restricted domain. What it was that broke the barrier I will never know—only that one night Tatyana suddenly called my attention to the fact that *Babushka* was tired and needed help. Her words might have been abrupt, but they were a welcomed, wonderful indication of her opening trust.

Babushka greeted me with a warm, knowing smile as pleased as I was, that "I had made it". She immediately opened up—laughing and chattering, and eager to show me everything that an American knew nothing about.

First she showed me how the spout of the tin water tank worked. That first night, she washed the dishes and I dried, after which we were joined by Tatyana who asked if I wanted to learn how to make bread. It was then, over a lump of dough the size of a small pig, that all the barriers went down. The dough was in an enormous bucket like those used for carrying fireplace ashes, though this was yellow with flowers on it. Using only a wooden instrument with a flat rectangular end, and not her hands, she mixed the dough into a smooth, perfect ball as if she had been mixing sour cream.

Now Nikolai, Tatyana, *Babushka* and I sat discussing the new library. Given that the books would most likely be used for decades, we decided to buy only the best we could find: the best paper and bindings, the best text, and the best balance of text and illustrations, even if that meant buying fewer books. *Babushka* got up to heat more water for tea while Tatyana told us of Vetoshkino's sister village, Votckoya. Votckoya was likewise settled in the 1800s, and its large graceful grade school still stood as a legacy of the beauty of the tsarist era.

The two-storied structure was now used in warmer

weather only. Like so many villages in Russia, the population was dwindling and the amount of work it took to keep the big school supplied with wood for fuel was now too much for two teachers and a director to keep up with on top of teaching.

A second, smaller, log cabin had been built opposite the main school and this was now used in winter. It, too, was heated with large wood burning stoves that stood like

faithful nannies in a corner of every classroom. The classrooms were no more than ten feet square and the green wooden desks noticeably smaller to fit the frames of little six, seven, and eight-year-olds. A paper alphabet of thirty-two letters hung next to each blackboard and, off to the side, a large red sign that said, "A century of living; a century of learning," or, more simply, "live to learn".

[Despite the fact that we learned about Votckoya only after we arrived in Vetoshkino, we still were able buy the school between 300 and 400 books. Unfortunately, the children were having their Easter break and so the little room where we sat was devoid of their laughter, and cold and unheated. Nonetheless, the school's two teachers and the director, Emelia Mikhailovna, had done their best to

make the day memorable. We sat in our coats and hats chatting happily, and then gathering here and there for photographs. They, too, would shower us with gifts—so dear, in some cases, that it was hard to accept them. Out of tattered cloth sacks they would draw exquisite handmade lace tablecloths and pillowcases, a small braided rug, and a delicate lace collar, old and irreplaceable. These had all been the work of their grandmothers, but laid in our hands without hesitation.]

Babushka returned with teapot in hand, obviously disappointed that our decisions had all been made and the discussion concluded. It was 1:00 a.m., Tatyana replied, time to take a stroll on the street (the Russian euphemism for visiting the outhouse) and to say good-night.

How to care for an American I later, sadly, learned, had caused Tatyana no small concern. There were not only the deep feminine feelings of what I would think of her home, but all the fears of how I would take to strolling on the street, chicken under feet, salted fish for breakfast—and the banya. Somewhat similar to a sauna, the banya is the way one bathes in the villages. To make *a good banya*, as they say, takes a considerable amount of work and so, much like laundry day, everyone gets washed, including neighbors who don't have a banya of their own. The men go in together when it is the hottest and most difficult to endure, after which the women take their turn. Nikolai, unbeknownst to me, had mentioned to Tatyana that he was concerned about how I would manage. Americans, he was quite sure, didn't bathe with others. They agreed, as a result, that I should learn alone with Tatyana.

Misha,* Sasha, and Nikolai returned from their banya as red as lobsters and eyed me rather intently as Tatyana led me across the courtyard to the adjoining small building. The first room was the same temperature as the out-

*Misha is the diminutive of Mikhail, and Sasha is the diminutive of Alexander.

side air and was where we were to undress, though I still didn't understand this. I was distracted by all the various objects: a large woodpile along the far wall, clothes lines crisscrossing the low ceiling, the numerous wash buckets, stacked here and there—and finally a thin wooden bench still wet.

Tatyana took the lead, undressing unselfconsciously. She nodded to me to move along quickly—though there was no need. Even with my clothes on I was freezing. To undress, I needed to remove my glasses. To my surprise, not being able to see Tatyana gave the illusion of her not being able to see me. Unfortunately, only now I realize I never told her how simple the solution to the problem of caring for an American in the banya turned out to be.

Tatyana opened the door into the second room and, without waiting, pushed me in. The steam felt like sharp needles. It was almost impossible to breathe. Off to the right I could see a large brick wood burning stove—the source of the intense heat. Wooden buckets, larger than any I had ever seen before, sat here and there filled with water of varying temperatures: scalding, warm, and cold.

"Are you O.K.? Can you breathe?" Tatyana kept asking sympathetically. If I got too hot, I was to pour buckets of cold water over myself. It would help me breathe more easily, she promised. It felt wonderful—and I now understood what drove Russians out into the snow to roll about.

At first, this large commanding woman had seemed stern. It is, however, a tradition of a Russian household.

She is the older sister here, and I the younger. She gives the orders, and I follow. It is she, however, who is responsible for everyone's needs, and I who am one of the beneficiaries of her caring: if I take off my hat outside, she quickly tells me to put it back on. Or it is she who makes sure no one gives me alcohol, and insists that I eat more.

"I'm fine Tatyana!" I replied rather loudly. The steam somehow made it seem as if you had to shout. With her every move I understood what a caring woman this was. She produced a basin and set it at my feet motioning me to put them into it. This, filled with water, brought a huge block of soap the color of beeswax floating to the surface. As I bent to wash my feet, she poured a bucket of steaming hot water on my back. "Don't worry!" she called out, You'll get used to it!" Two, three, four more buckets of hot water came cascading over my head before she began to beat my back with moist, sweet smelling leafy branches. This ritual was called *paritsa* and, to most Russians, the nearest thing to heaven itself.

Finally, I was ordered to wash my hair while Tatyana at last took care of herself. Off to my right there was a wooden shelf with several bottles and containers on it. There even appeared to be someone's toothbrush. Next to it, the shape of a blue and white bottle caught my eye. "It *must* be the shampoo," I thought to myself, "even in a banya in the middle of nowhere, in a world that still resembles Tolstoy's—a plastic bottle must be the shampoo!" It was.

The wet rectangular bottle said, *Head and Shoulders.*

The second layer

We left for Kirov on a sunny, Friday morning. Mikhail left before us in his jeep, pulling a trailer full of beef. If he sold it all by noon, he would then meet us to help collect and bring the books home. The two and a half hour drive north landed us in Kirov just as the shops were opening. The time had now arrived for me to learn the ways of the Russian marketplace.

I knew already that one of the most important things to understand about Russia is its deeply held traditions —the living of thousands of innate customs that constitute the fabric of both friendship and society. Nikolai had even once remarked that traditions were still the strongest influence in Russian society, far more so than the rule of law or democracy would ever be—simply because traditions are trusted, and rule of law is not.

Even names are a complex way by which one shows understanding and respect. At different times, Nikolai, for example, might be referred to in any one of five ways:

> Nikolai Mikailovich Arjannikov,
> Nikolai Mikailovich,
> Mikhailich,
> Nikolai,
> or simply Kolya.

The first is used primarily for official documents. The second and third are more subtle. They are used as not only a sign of respect, but to convey one's understanding of the appropriate tone of a particular conversation. The name Nikolai is rarely used on its own, as friends use the most informal name of Kolya.*

Without understanding at least the most basic traditions, the chances of an American working effectively in Russia would be severely handicapped. These traditions, founded on the basis of respect and as old as Russia itself, were not to be disregarded, for they would make it much easier for a foreigner to gain access into a Russian heart, home, or marketplace.

The shopkeeper of the small bookstore on the busy main street of Kirov, even though properly greeted, was, for some reason, unusually stony-faced and reserved. It was surprising given that Nikolai and Tatyana had made it plain that we were going to buy a considerable number of books. The short, plump dour faced clerk stood unimpressed, as well as unmoved, behind a horseshoe shaped counter that separated us from her—as well as from the books themselves.

Tatyana read a number of the titles we were looking for, and Nikolai explained that we wanted only books of the best quality. Still none of this caused any real response. The one or two she produced were only of average quality at best. They could not have withstood long-term use. Seeing at last that they would have to take a more patient, coaxing tack, Nikolai and Tatyana began to explain the

*Nikolai's mother had once said to me, "Nikolai is just a name. It doesn't tell you anything."

library project. Did she know the village of Vetoshkino?

Well, yes, she had heard of it, but she didn't know anyone who lived there. What were the roads like now?

Still very bad.

Would all the books be used in the library?

Yes, except the ones to be given to each child to have for his or her own. She could look at the list herself.

This second wave of effort produced only a minimal result and Nikolai, losing patience, decided it was time to intimate that she was bordering on insulting his integrity. He definitely would buy books from her, he carefully explained, only if she was willing to tell us where in town we could buy books of the highest quality. He knew, he continued, that such books obviously existed, and he was determined (as his voice and demeanor now made plain) to have nothing but the very best for these children.

Finally she believed him. It had taken nearly an hour, but when we had earned her trust, she was suddenly able to supply us with literally hundreds of *beautiful* books.

The bookshelves, I soon learned, consisted of not one, but two layers—the front layer, immediately visible to the customer, being books of average and inexpensive quality. These, however, the shopkeeper suddenly began to take down revealing a second layer of books, hidden from view, of astonishing quality. They were as beautiful and of as fine a quality as any hardbound volume you could find in Moscow, London, Boston, or New York. So why on earth—let alone here in this remote city—were they hidden? Because you had to convince the store owners that their most treasured books would be truly valued and well used before they'd let them go. The best books were not about making money. They were about the value of books themselves and how they would be used.

We would have a similar experience at the second bookstore, but here the bookshelves were accessible to the customers themselves and the atmosphere less restrictive. With the exception of one or two books, by the end of the day we had found beautiful editions of every child's request, as well as art and science books, full sets of encyclopedias, Russian-English dictionaries, all the literary classics, and whatever else struck us as of value.

For the main school in Vetoshkino we bought nearly 1000 books—including the children's gift books. Sergei Evgenevich had also asked if it might be possible to buy the school a television set, VCR, and educational videos. These were found—along with a copy of Walt Disney's *Babe*. The talking pig, I promised, was truly inspiring.

There was only one final task to be accomplished. We returned to the second bookstore where, earlier in the day, Nikolai had asked the owner to show him her two most beautiful books. They were to be gifts for the directors of the two village schools. Did she have any special hardbound editions of Mikhail Bulgakov's famed *Master and Marguerita*? She shook her head. Unfortunately, it was hard to find such things here in Kirov. Maybe Moscow, but not Kirov. Nikolai didn't press the point but let the subject drop.

It was now past closing time. We had come to collect

all the packed up boxes of books and, while Tatyana and I helped the clerks, again Nikolai approached the owner of the store, quietly and alone. It was very important to him, he explained, to honor these two dedicated people. Could she really not help him? . . .

There were, in fact, she finally confessed, two editions of *Master and Marguerita* in the store, but they were her prized possessions. She brought them out and carefully laid them on the counter. They stared at them for a long time. The books were truly exquisite. It was understandable, Nikolai said, why no one would want to part with them. She then looked up at him and smiled. She would gift wrap them, she said at last, if he liked.

"Today," Nikolai Mikhailovich was always saying, "is when you must do your very best. You will never get the

chance to live today again." His hand was on his chest as he thanked the shopkeeper again, and again, and again. He even bowed slightly as we left. He walked down the street oblivious to everything around him. The experience was a rare one for an American to see, and a glimpse of something purely Russian. These last two books, and what they represented, were as important to Nikolai as the hundreds we bought that day. Life was not business. It was life itself, and that meant that it was to be lived at its most beautiful.

We spoke very little during the car ride home. No one wanted to disturb Nikolai. In the silence, I thought of children poring over "Gemingway" and Shakespeare, and and all the Russian greats. "Words are sacred." I had read once somewhere. "If you get the right ones in the right order, you can nudge the world a little."

Before we left Vetoshkino, Nikolai gave Mikhail some money and asked that the next time he went to Kirov to please buy the shopkeeper the most beautiful armful of flowers that had ever been grown.

A day to celebrate!

The twenty-third of March became a holiday, even if only to be celebrated once—and despite the grey clouds overhead and the cold slush beneath our feet. Everyone happily and noisily unloaded the books, oblivious to both the weather outside and the quickly changing conditions in Sergei Evgenevich's office who could no longer reach his desk for all the boxes. Along with Sergei Evgenevich and his wife Olga Anatolevna—the schoolteachers, Tatyana,

Mikhail, Sasha, and his sweet young girlfriend Luba had all eagerly come to help.

Once all the boxes had been carted inside, the books themselves began to be unpacked and opened as carefully as if they had been made of glass. Hands ran over the pages in silence, the teachers' faces saying more than could be said in any language. At last, Nikolai unpacked "the prize," a magnificent *World Atlas* that was over two and a half feet tall and held in a beautiful slip case. None of us had ever seen a more beautiful book. Sergei Evgenevich resolved that the atlas would have a table of its own. No child would be able to lift it and, laying on a table, they would feel like they could climb into it. We hovered over it like Columbuses discovering the world. Almost immediately someone said, "Find the page with North America." It was found, and then my small home town. It was only a spot on a map—but somehow it felt like we were there. Their faces lit up at the sound of the lyrical names of towns and lakes—all of which were native American.

The atlas's pale green silk ribbon was put in the page to show the children when they returned from their Easter holiday. Then Sergei Evgenevich pulled Nikolai to him and held him tightly to his chest. He then came to me and held both of my hands in his. His eyes said everything.

We returned home and suddenly everyone began to bustle about as if it was Christmas Eve. *"Shashlik!"* everyone kept calling out merrily to one another. I wasn't quite sure what it meant but, given the preparations, it was safe to assume it meant we were going to celebrate. The jeep was carefully backed up to the courtyard gate. The trunk was flipped open and the seats folded first down, and then back up, while firewood and axes, long scarves and warm hats, and several pairs of heavy black *valenki* were assigned to their places. Huge sacks of bread and cheese began to appear, followed by large jars of pickled cucumbers, mushrooms and beets, and, at last, a bucket of tender chunks of beef. With a smile and a wink, Mikhail invited me into the front seat. As always, Tatyana was the last one out the door, making sure we had forgotten nothing.

It was going on five o'clock. We had to move along before it got too dark to find just the right spot. The car climbed up hill and down, everyone gesturing, pointing,

and discussing the advantages of this place or that. At last, we rounded a bend and there on a gently rising slope sat a little clump of pine and birch trees. It was gorgeous.

Where else but Russia, I thought laughingly to myself, would people celebrate in midwinter—in the middle of the woods! Now I understood. *Shashlik* didn't mean "a day to celebrate," it meant "barbecue".

The men went first, carrying the axes and wood, and buckets of meat. They would go ahead, tramping down the snow, clearing a path and a place for us to set up. The clump of trees, we soon discovered, had a small natural clearing of its own. It couldn't have been more beautiful. Sasha, Mikhail, and Nikolai danced around like Indian chiefs until content that the snow was packed enough so that we wouldn't fall in up to our hips. Then Mikhail set to making a fire with the logs and kindling we had taken with us. "One log" Nikolai called out happily, heading off with Sasha to cut down bench trees, "cannot start a fire! It takes all of us working together." His smile was huge.

Soon we could hear the rhythm of axes swinging and slicing into the base of trees—until there was that final crack, the brushing of branches, and a soft thud into the snow below. Three small trees, de-limbed and cleared of snow, were set up for benches. A larger one was used to prepare the food on. Tatyana began to mix a sauce into the tub of meat while Luba and I put the chunks on long steel skewers. All the while the fire grew larger, brighter, and warmer. "There needs to be enough coals," Mikhail explained, "to last until midnight! . . ."

Sasha headed off in the jeep to collect Tatyana's sister and brother-in-law who were to join the festivities. The sun had long ago set but the night air was gentle, and the fire roaring. The conversation flowed like water between stories and songs, one spilling after another like verse and chorus. A bottle of vodka was opened—but not without Mikhail's surprising me with a large bottle of lemonade. Tatyana smiled in approval and shared it with me.

The tall narrow pines led your eye naturally upward to the sky. It had cleared now, and though there was a gentle haze around the moon, the stars were sparkling and showing through. The happy, contented evening passed all too soon but, true to their word, it was after midnight when the fire finally died out. We gathered the axes and empty cloth sacks. There was not room now in the jeep for all of us and, as it was a quiet, lovely night, Nikolai, Tatyana, and I were just as happy to walk. Only later did I learn what Nikolai had been thinking about in the stillness during the peaceful walk home: to him, every new library was like a road begun. What pleased him most, was that *all the people who had helped us*, not just he and I and Tatyana, were walking down the road together.

"The longest road," says the Russian proverb, "begins with the first step." Like the road that stretched before us in the stillness of the night, neither we, nor any of the dear people who had helped us, would ever see where one small remote library would lead. It was something you choose to do without being able to see the effects. That the road was simply *there* meant that others would travel farther.

POSTSCRIPT: VETOSHKINO

7 August 2002
Vetoshkino, Russia

Greetings, dear Jeannie!

A huge thank you for your letters! I wrote you long ago, but the letter remains here in Vetoshkino. The next time Sasha goes to Kirov he will mail that one and this for me. He and Luba are home from school until September 1st and are helping tend the cows.

It has been six months since your visit, yet the children in the village even now always talk about it and thank you and your friends. With great pleasure they are reading their books and remembering you and Kolya. It is still hard to believe that such a thing could have happened to us.

When I tell the children that you ask about them they are amazed that you are still remembering us. Sergei Evgenevich and Olga Anatolevna are anxious to write you. We wait from you your next letter.

Until then Jeannie, Tatyana

PERVOURALSK, THE URAL MOUNTAINS

PART II
GENTLY COME, GENTLY GO

Siberia
4 April 2002

It is early morning. Judging by the sky and the thick frost on the window it is below zero; colder than usual for this time of year. The view has a truly Siberian feel to it (or at least what people who've never been here before always *imagine* Siberia to be like). Houses, fence posts, and the still untrodden road all have a fresh coat of snow. The air is moist and filled with soft shades of pink.

The window has a thick coat of ice as the inside shutters were closed last night. When they're latched, a shelf below the window can be lifted to let in more heat from the radiator. This room is separate from the main house and not heated by the wood stove. The house is the seventh brown one on *Vasilovskovor Street*, with pale blue shutters—and is where Nikolai was born and raised. The table where I sit has two *cymdukes*, or wooden trunks, on either side, each covered with a thick oriental rug to make them more comfortable for sitting on. They hold treasures of earlier days: heavy blue and white tapestry bed coverings (exactly like those in Vetoshkino), handmade pillow cases and table-cloths, and several delicate white lace collars.

I imagine the stories the writing table could tell of all

that's happened over the years. Some stories, however, will never be told, stories, for instance, about the "Siberian Trek," as it's called, a road less than a mile from here over which so many walked to their exile. Nikolai pointed it out but said very little, only that one must consider it to understand the country. Now it borders a woods. There is little to see, except in your imagination. Other than Nikolai, people are reluctant to talk of political matters. It is not a case of avoiding anything, just a yearning for others to know something more about this country.

War turned these mountains into a hidden factory in 1943. It was one of the miracles of World War II. The first factories made truck parts. People worked in them all day, and then three more hours each night constructing new factories that today still number in the hundreds. Women were given two weeks' leave after having a baby.

Zoya Fedorovna Arjannikov gave forty-five years to the town's hospital as a medical assistant while raising her two sons, Vasily and Nikolai. She comes in every morning to tell me when Nikolai is up and dressed. She knows she will find me writing, nonetheless she will say,

"*Melaiya*, (dear) are you writing so soon? It is time for breakfast." As she turns to go out she will quietly say, "*Melaiya*, the people, write about the people."

The other face of communism

The journey from Vetoshkino to Pervouralsk was long,

but uneventful, other than the discussion. For most of the eighteen hour drive it had been devoted to discussing the Soviet Union, communism, war, propaganda, and God.

I remember nothing about the passing landscape, only that around 10:00 p.m. Nikolai said we had just crossed the border where Europe meets Asia. Less than a mile later we turned into his driveway.

The house was dark as his mother had already gone to bed. He hadn't told her exactly when we'd be arriving. ("How could I know? This is Russia!")

It was only with some difficulty, because of the snow, that Nikolai got the gate of the picket fence open. He went to the far left front window, knocked three times and waited. A light came on, followed moments later by a light in the middle two windows, and finally the sound of a door opening and feet shuffling across the crunching snow. I waited back by the car to let Nikolai greet her first. When the courtyard door swung open, my first thought was how small she looked in comparison with it, and how very childlike she was. To my surprise Nikolai stood back, neither hugging nor kissing her, though they stared into each other's eyes a long time. At last he gently said hello and called after me to come meet her. Her face was as if sunlight had been shining on it. It was lit with a warm, embracing smile. There was no waiting to get to know her. She just took me in, as she did everyone.

"Why, Nikolai," I later asked, knowing the closeness of Russian families, "didn't you kiss your mother hello?"

"I rarely know when I'll be home," he began. "To

make it less difficult for her, I leave as if I'll be back in an hour, and return as if there's been no separation. It's easier if it's less emotional. Gently come. Gently go."

Over long days, lengthy discussions, and 4000 miles of road, Nikolai would show me things about Russia that made me realize how very little is known of this country, and how much that *is* known is strangely deprived of its meaning. It was never an effort to convince me of anything, but to let me see what there was to be seen, and to then let me come to my own conclusions. Scenes etched themselves in my memory: the *endless* snow covered earth with a single road on it, no other cars, no signs, no homes, no stray dogs, no towns. Suddenly, a lone woman would be walking with a child at her side, and one in her arms. *Where had they come from? How far were they going?* My eyes would strain looking for another road, a town, or a home. Or there would be the slogans, or huge initials of the U.S.S.R., permanently held in brick patterns on the sides of buildings in the smallest, most remote towns.

"When they were put there no one ever dreamed it could fall apart," Nikolai explained as we drove through a town where he noticed me staring at such a building, "anymore than you can fathom the end of the U.S." He then stared at me intently to see if I could fathom such a thing. Did I now better understand just how dramatic the collapse had been for Russians?

Rarely would Nikolai approach the subject of communism in terms of whether it was right or wrong. It was, rather, simply what people *believed.*

"The communist ideal was the most incredible of all Russian fairy tales: promising a world of happiness, well being, equality, justice, and all that would make life meaningful. If such a world seemed far off after years of effort, you still worked for it, thinking that at least it would be so for your children. People only slowly faced the fact that this tale would never be. They wanted to believe that such a world was possible. They wanted to believe that if it had not been reached it wasn't communism that had failed—but simply themselves. When the illusion ended, it was like a narcotic wearing off. We were left with nothing but the same yearning for a better life.

"To understand Russia, is like opening a safe. It takes turning the combination lock in many ways. Only one turn of the combination is communism. There are the dissidents, war, our culture and literature, our traditions, our history—as well as all those things that Westerners think of when they think of Russia: the K.G.B., vodka, balalaika music, and *matrushka* dolls.

"It isn't really a question of whether I love Russia or not. I cannot decide whether or not I love my hand or my leg. It is simply mine, what I was given."

Neither Nikolai, his friends, his little mother, nor her large sister-in-law, whose name also happens to be Zoya, act anything like "communists". As for what these good simple people with their fine hair, mended sweaters, and warm bulky fur hats *think*—they think that I act nothing like a "capitalist".

In an eager show of friendship, one friend had given me his Soviet military hat the night Nikolai's friends came to welcome him home. Vladimir has the most wonderful laugh. It shakes his whole body, as well as anything in the near proximity—a table, teacup, or friend.

It had been arranged that Vladimir would pick us up the following night at 10:00 p.m. Our car, the day after we arrived, broke down and was with a repairman who lived about forty minutes away. Five minutes out of town we left all semblance of recognizable roads and were merrily driving over six months of packed ice and snow.

I was leaning forward in the middle of the backseat to hear better the conversation in the front. I couldn't help but think what a good hearted soul this Vladimir was. He had worked hard all day and now had come out late, and in the cold, to help us. After he dropped us off he would have almost an hour's ride home again all alone.

For some ten years Vladimir and his wife, Nadershda, have worked to build a house and barn. The barn is done and home to a mother cow, her new calf, and several chickens. Though covered seven months of the year in snow, the vegetable garden produces enough to keep them most of the year. A beehive keeps them in honey and one finished room in the house keeps them warm. Depending on the hour, it serves as kitchen, living room, or bedroom. They are neither rich nor poor. They're Russian—and as a result, helping a friend is as expected as the sunrise, even if the gas tank is on *empty*.

The little red fuel indicator glowed as brightly as any new Christmas tree light. The tank was as empty as the fields around us. I tried not to think about it. The miles dragged on. The car crawled over each ice rut in the road. Vladimir would gun the engine to get us out. By the time we reached the repairman's house I was exhausted. The house sat on top of the garage where our car sat waiting for us. Unable to knock on the window, Vladimir stood below bellowing, "Eh, Mikhailich! It's me . . . Vladimir! Open up!" While the chorus went on, I reached over the seat tugging at Nikolai's sleeve. *Nety!* "No more!" I said frantically, pointing at the gauge. He understood.

"Eh, Vladimir!" Nikolai now began to bellow out the car window. With characteristic sensitivity, given that his friend's pockets were very likely also on empty, Nikolai continued, "Jeannie's upset that your car doesn't have any gas. She doesn't know that's normal! It's impossible to teach her everything at once. Do you mind if we go get some?" We tandemed to a gas station with Vladimir in front. He jumped out as the car coasted to a stop. Puffs of frosty breath escaped from beneath his gorgeous black moustache as he held his sides and laughed.

Aunty Zoya, on the other hand, was happiest overseeing a table piled high with food and people eating. The more you ate the better, and if you didn't eat enough she would begin to check for early signs of illness. The word "full" was not in her vocabulary. Fortunately, Aunty Zoya was not there the morning Mother Zoya filled my plate with a huge fish head. "I saved it for you," she said. "It's the best part! *Kyshaietiya.* Eat up!" It was eight o'clock. I shot Nikolai a desperate glance as soon as Mama went back to the kitchen. Without hesitation, he forked the salted creature in one deft move and consumed it.

When Aunty Zoya arrived, Nikolai announced that he thought we should call her sister who lived in faraway Kiev. The rare, unexpected call proved to be emotional.

"Don't cry, Vera! Please don't cry! We have only a few minutes. Tell me how you are. Don't cry! It's not necessary, Vera. I am always remembering you."

Vera was all her life an invalid and housebound. Both sisters were now pensioners and unable to pay for either a train ticket or a simple phone call.

This Russia, which was forever separating loved ones and bringing new partings (as well as the consciousness that nothing on earth is more dear than those who are so far), this Russia was one that I had read much about, but had not *felt* until sitting in the midst of a small chapter of a family story. I leaned over to Nikolai and whispered, "Do you think they will ever see each other again?"

"*Net.*"

"Do they know that?"

"*Da.*"

The phone had already been returned to its holder, while Nikolai added, "The transition to democracy has been the most difficult for our parents. Suddenly Zoya's sister lives in a different country [Ukraine]. She needs a passport to visit her and doesn't know why. Traveling is expensive and dangerous, as well. Where is her freedom?"

Before she left to go home, Nikolai gave Aunty Zoya money for a train ticket. She burst into tears saying she couldn't accept it. It was too much. She couldn't take so much money from him; but at last she did. Nonetheless the look in her eyes was one of sadness.

In the morning Aunty Zoya returned with the money. "I will never forget," she said with tears in her eyes. Her health was not up to the trip, she said. Later, Nikolai told me the real reason. Her husband forbade her. It was far away and war was still raging in Chechnya.

In Aunty Zoya's hand was also a little pair of blue and grey striped knitted socks. "Try them!" she said with a courageous smile. They were like something a Dr. Seuss character might be found wearing. They were absolutely wonderful. "But how did you know the size!?" I asked.

"I looked at your hands, of course!" She patted my hand as she spoke.

In the days ahead, Nikolai would privately arrange to pay the phone company an extra sum. Aunty Zoya could at least call her sister once more.

Nikolai continues the conversation

"In Russia there is a saying, *Leesh bwe ne bwila vainah.*

'Life may be awful, but at least it's not war. Let us endure anything, but not war.' If our children are taught a very different view of war than your children—and that even, for example, that Russia was responsible for winning the war [World War II]—you must understand how we count the cost of that war. Let us say that one American family contributed five dollars and lost one son in the war, and that one Russian family gave one dollar and lost five sons. Who gave more to win the war?"*

When the fathers and sons never returned, it was the mothers of Russia who were left to calculate, and remember, the real cost of the war.

Zoya Fedorovna was a student in high school studying medicine when the war broke out. She was living in Vetoshkino where she had been born seventeen years earlier. All students were called to Sovietskoya that summer to expedite their studies. They studied ten hours a day, six days a week. At night, Zoya studied by kerosene lamp as there was no electricity. She received a stipend of thirty-five rubles a month for being a medical student, and the family of eight still had their father's small pension. (He had died a year before the war broke out.)

"We grew vegetables. By comparison, we were fortunate. But there was nothing in the village to buy. We carried things like flour, soap, matches, and kerosene from Sovietskoya. We'd start out every Saturday night at 10:00 carrying as much as possible. We wouldn't reach the village until around 10:00 the next morning. The walk from Sovietskoya to Vetoshkino was forty-five miles.

*In the battle of Stalingrad alone, Russia lost more soldiers than all the allied forces lost in the entire war.

"Mother would have the banya ready for me to warm my cold legs and bathe. We'd have to return again that evening. Mother would send me back with bread and hard-boiled eggs. We'd get back in time for class Monday morning. In summer we wore *laptee* on the road [see photograph on page iv], and in winter, *valenki*. At school we were given canvas shoes, they even had heels.

"In 1945 [at 21] I went to work in the Infants' Home. There were many children's homes in the villages. Train loads of children had been sent from Leningrad to the villages to be cared for until the end of the war. I was both the director and sole doctor. It was very difficult. I would write the school asking for advice. They would send back detailed letters.

"People were so strong then. I've never forgotten one woman. Her time had come. Usually women had their children at home, but she was having trouble. It was May 2nd, *rasputeetza*.* The roads had disappeared. There was nothing but mud everywhere. I knew at once that I had to get her to the hospital. The closest one was ten miles away. The poor woman had already traveled three miles. Her young son had run beside the cart pulling the horse. The horse was old and worn out and the mud very deep.

"I sent the boy to a village about a mile down the road to find another horse. He returned with a pair of horses and we started out. Again, he ran along beside them urging them forward. It was both raining and snowing. The woman was crying out terribly. The child was coming. I told the boy to stop and I began to prepare. I got out alco-

*The word literally means, "the time of bad roads".

hol and iodine and washed my hands. I implored the son to hold the blanket and shield his mother from the wind. She barely cried; just, 'Lord, help.' I reached my hand into the womb. As if someone was prompting me, I found and took hold of the child's heel.

"So came the first child. As I tied the umbilical cord, the second child came out of his own accord. I put the babies on their mother's breast and covered her up from the cold and the wind, and we went on to the hospital. They reprimanded me when they saw that I had not tied the umbilical cords properly. When they saw how young I was, they assumed I had been careless and irresponsible. When they learned that I had delivered the children in a field, in the snow, they were speechless.

"As the war went on, there was nothing, simply *nothing*. All but the oldest men were all gone. The cows and horses and chickens were all gone. Only old horses were left. When they were finally gone, the old men and little boys were left to pull the carts.

"Eventually we had no milk for the children and not even any tea. We made soup from grass and leaves. The children were always hungry. Winter was particularly difficult. Once a week we'd wash their clothes. They only had one set and so they'd sit naked on the stove all day to keep warm until their clothes were clean and dry. It was so difficult if an epidemic broke out. I would walk home at night crying. It was so difficult to sort things out."

Nikolai, Tatyana, and I had driven to Sovietskoya on

the last day of *Maslenetsya*, the festive holiday when winter is sent away with bonfires, singing and dancing. The town bears a lovely rural beauty bordering on elegance. The streets are lined with wooden homes trimmed with finely carved finials, rafters, rake boards, and shutters— all in soft Russian shades of yellow, blue, and green. Red geraniums, or contented cats, sit in the windows. The town gives no evidence of the days when once only young girls, who had no time to dream of love and marriage, or sentimental things, could be seen on the streets, having walked all night to get there.

Now a market stands in the center of the town filled with makeshift stalls and rickety wooden tables piled high with handmade wares: balls of knobby, dark grey wool, thick, white knitted winter socks, woven baskets, whisk brooms, *valenki*, hats, and scarves.

One woman was standing next to a small table. Did I know what she was selling, Nikolai asked, pointing to the large metal bucket she was tending? He reached in his pocket fishing for five kopecks, in exchange for which she gave us a cleverly folded triangular cup made from the pages of an old book. It was filled with sunflower seeds. This was a Russian version of a popcorn vender and business was brisk. Tatyana could husk and eat the seeds, and spit out the shell using only her tongue and teeth.

Our seeds were being held in page 312 of some thus plucked and now pageless book. We got a conversation between Konstantine Sergeevich and Pavel Ivanovich.

Nikolai and Tatyana only laughed when I told them

I wanted to keep the packet. As for the rest of the pages, they would end crumpled in people's pockets, Pavel and Konstantine doomed for the wood stove—rather than a shelf in America. My thoughts have often gone back to the *babushkas* selling their grey balls of wool, knobby knitted socks, and packets of seed. Beneath their heavy aged forms are women who once did astonishing things. I picture them walking over the road. I inevitably feel ashamed that I fell asleep in the car driving home.

Ekaterinburg

By contrast, Ekaterinburg, the tsarist era city of the Urals, had a market equal to Moscow's famed Arbat Street, the treelined promenade filled with talented merchants and accomplished artists. Here you can find exquisitely made birch bark boxes along side highly polished and decorated stone eggs, Soviet era souvenirs on top of tsarist era antiques, shiny samovars next to faded prayer books, as well as silent, melancholy icons, and old accordions.

What was noticeably absent from the city were the typical, grey, faceless block buildings of the communist era. Impressive museums and huge universities lined the bustling streets where, despite the bitter cold, Nikolai and I, and our close friend Anatoly, were strolling. My companions had proudly pointed out the central library, the

Military Institute, and Ural State University (one of fourteen universities), the railway station and opera house, as well as the many beautiful monuments. In fact, all this was far too beautiful, it seemed to me, to have been communist. As if reading my mind, Nikolai looked over at me and said, "This, too, is what communism gave us."

Anatoly was tempted to buy nothing in the market, while Nikolai found an old silver soup spoon that he wore sticking out of the chest pocket of his winter coat. Only one girl, a pleasant clerk in a computer store, asked him why he went about town with a silver soup spoon in his chest pocket. "To be always ready for dinner...."

When we left the busy upscale store, my jovial companions (missing the irony of their question) continued, "Do you know why we were taught to view capitalists as criminals? We were taught that life was about good work and not about making money. If you bought something from someone and turned around and sold it at a higher price, you were thrown in prison. You were considered a common thief because you'd used someone else's hard work and benefited from it. You wanted money, but you didn't want to work for it."

Anatoly, amused at his own candor, said that in all his life he never dreamed an American would just "turn over funds" without dictating how *every kopeck* must be spent. He was referring to our first library project.

What I didn't admit to Anatoly, thinking back to that first project, was that I never thought Russians could be so dependable and trustworthy. Anatoly and Vladimir had both helped Nikolai launch our first library in January 2001 at the Middle School of Pervouralsk where they had all gone to school together. None of them had taken a cent for their help, but had wholeheartedly plunged into the project, helping to buy, and then transport, over 800 new library books—200 more than we had expected to buy. Time and again I would see how much good work clearly meant to them, whether it was a beautiful old soup spoon, a new library for children, or the latest capitalistic laptop computer.

Tireless lives

There were two tubs. One was plastic, long and white, and about a foot deep. In it, you washed the clothes and rinsed them. The other was about three feet in diameter and made of tin. It held clean hot water (heated on the stove) and was used for each new rinsing. The narrow, toothed washboard was different from those that are now used here *only in museums*. But the heavy, square block of dull yellow-green soap was instantly recognizable.

About 10:00 p.m. one evening, when Nikolai was out, I gathered a small armful of dirty clothes and headed for the kitchen where the only sink was located. You always had to be alert coming or going from the kitchen because of the heavy trap door in the middle of the floor that let you down into the root cellar below.

The root cellar was a wonder. It was filled with huge

one and two gallon jars of pickles, beets, and mushrooms. There were even larger jars of apple, and cherry juice, as well as sacks of potatoes, carrots, and turnips. The outside shed held frozen chickens and stiff salted fish.

Mother Zoya Fedorovna was just emerging from the root cellar as I was coming through with my laundry. To get into the cellar you had to jump down about three and a half feet on to a stone platform. From there, there were four wooden steps into the cellar itself. Zoya Fedorovna leaped into the cellar as agilely as any child. Considering that the floor onto which she had to pull herself out again was up to her chest—she got out even more remarkably. She was just pulling herself out as I was coming through. She took in the situation immediately and scurried to the courtyard to get the tubs.

I assured her nothing so fancy was necessary, holding up my little white bottle of expensive *Fabric Care Wash* that a friend had given me just before I left. Mother Zoya Fedorovna, however, was not impressed with either the cost, or the size, of the small white bottle. Where was the soap?

"This is soap!"

It took well over an hour just to wash the clothes with the yellow-green soap, and the hard part was yet to come. Two kitchen chairs had been pulled together to set the wash basin on. It still meant working with a bent back which Mother Zoya could fully sympathize with after so many years. She sat on the third chair both instructing

and encouraging me to get the clothes *cleaner*. I made the mistake of leaving a heavy, red corduroy dress, and a pair of new black jeans for last. Washing them, however, was the least of it. Zoya Fedorovna's rule was that the clothes must be rinsed and wrung however many times it took until the water remained as clear as before you put them into it. After every rinsing I lugged the heavy white tub of water outside across the snow behind the outhouse to dump it. In the cold and dark you could see many things more clearly. Silent figures from a book read once long ago rose up and came alive in my mind: a group of peasant women in winter, bent over, wrapped in their heavy coats and padded leggings, their hands red, numb, rinsing laundry in a lake through a hole in the ice.

I now, too, saw how tireless Zoya Fedorovna was.

In Russia, everything is difficult, but everything is possible

I opened the shutter at the sound of all the noise. It was overcast. The road had turned to slush. Six teenage boys were pushing an old yellow Lada up the road, making little headway. Younger boys darted in and out, got in the way and shouted—and sometimes contributed an occasional push. The car was pathetic even by Russian standards. I couldn't see who they were helping.

Three days later, we happened to be coming home as the car was again being pushed up the road, only this time in the opposite direction. There were the same group of boys, all shoving it through the slush and snow with the same amount of Herculean effort. As we passed I caught sight of the poor "owner". This time, it was a laughing boy of nine or ten taking his turn "driving".

Mother Zoya Fedorovna had neither a car nor a banya which meant, in order to bathe, she walked to the home of Mikhail and Nadershda. They lived over a mile away with their son, and his eight-year-old son, Zhenya.

Two or three days after arriving in Pervouralsk they invited us over for borsch and a good banya—neither of which were ever to be turned down. Anatoly, who also doesn't have a banya, had been invited as well, and came to get us in his little white Lada. Nikolai's older brother, Vasily, showed up shortly after Anatoly pulled in the driveway. Thrilled with his fortuitous timing he eagerly joined the group. When we at last managed to squeeze everyone (along with sacks of towels and fresh clothes) in the car, the merry atmosphere felt peculiarly like heading off to a Thanksgiving dinner.

While waiting for the men to finish their long banya, Zhenya and I struck up a friendship over his multicolored rabbit's foot. Without thinking, I asked him to show me his favorite toy. When he answered by saying that he didn't have one, I suddenly realized that the small box of things he had pulled out to show me was the extent of his toys. The very next moment, he glanced up to see his grandmother fixing a plate of pickles and, without being asked, leaped up to help her. He would occasionally look over his shoulder to see if I was noticing how carefully he was arranging them on the plate.

He was an incredibly good little boy, which was why everyone was surprised when he flatly refused to go with his grandfather to have his banya. It was clear that this was totally unexpected behavior from him. Mikhail only shook his head and went off alone. Finally, the evening drew to a close and Mama Zoya got up to refill our sacks with wet towels and soiled clothes. In a flash, Zhenya was up and dashing out the room. Nadershda only shook her head saying she didn't know what had gotten into him. When we opened the courtyard gate, Zhenya was waiting by the car. He took off at full pace. How hard he tried to run as fast as he could—smiling and looking over his shoulder to see if we were noticing. Slowly, the car gained on him. *"Faster, Zhenya, faster!"* we called out. He beamed proudly. Happy now, he was ready for his banya.

A couple of days later, while his grandmother was visiting Zoya Fedorovna, I pulled out one of the children's books I had brought with me and asked her to give it to him. We had not only purchased books in Russia for the library, but I had taken a few of my favorite children's stories with me that a Russian friend had helped me translate. *The Big Hungry Bear* in hand, Zhenya's grandmother headed home as happily as if the book was her own.

The long walk in winter to Mikhail's and Nadershda's was becoming difficult for Zoya Fedorovna. Nikolai very much wanted to build her a banya. It weighed terribly on him and, as a result, in a uniquely Russian way, weighed on his friends. It was built in the spring just weeks after I left. When the last board was nailed in place, they all carved their names in it. The banya, by careful design, was exactly seven steps from the end of Nikolai's bed.

Nikolai shared his small room with his grandmother until her passing. Once a week Anna Kirilovna, who was unable to read or write, sat at the table at the end of the room and dictated a letter to her grandson. The letter to her sister was always the same. Nothing about it ever varied. As he repeated it to me, his voice was filled with the same labor of the young boy trying to write it long ago.

My dear Sister Olga Kirilovna ~

Tell me, how are you? How are Alosha, Misha, Sasha, Zhana, Tanya, and Vanya? How is Babushka Maria Fedorovna? Please send my greetings to Irina Petrovna, Elena Ivanova, Zoya Mikhailovna, Olga Andreevna, Natalia Sergeevna, Stepan Stepanovich, Vladimir Vladimirvich, the brothers Konstantine and Sergei Ivanovich, Yury Mikhailovich, Anatoly Anatolevich, Igor Petrovich, and Sofia Sergeevich. My health remains poor. Zoya works hard. Kolya is a good boy. I am never forgetting any of you. I await your answer like the nightingale of summer.*

~Your Sister Anna Kirilovna

*This old Russian ending was heartfelt. Letters from loved ones were as dear as the nightingale's song.

When the letter was finished, Nikolai would have to read it back to his grandmother to make sure he had not left out anyone's name. Then Anna Kirilovna would get up and get him a spoonful of homemade jam.

As I had been given Nikolai's room to use, he was left to sleep atop the stove. The narrow, six rung ladder takes

you up to a thick mat overlaid with a quilt and, as always, there are two enormous pillows. As in Vetoshkino, the stove is the center of the house, around which everything else is set.

The teal blue family room has three, rather than two, large windows that flood the room, the sofa, and Zoya Fedorovna's little cat, with light. The cat occupies the end of the sofa closest to the window which leaves the other end free for sitting and looking at television or old photographs.

This room, too, has a writing table, an oak *schkaf*, or

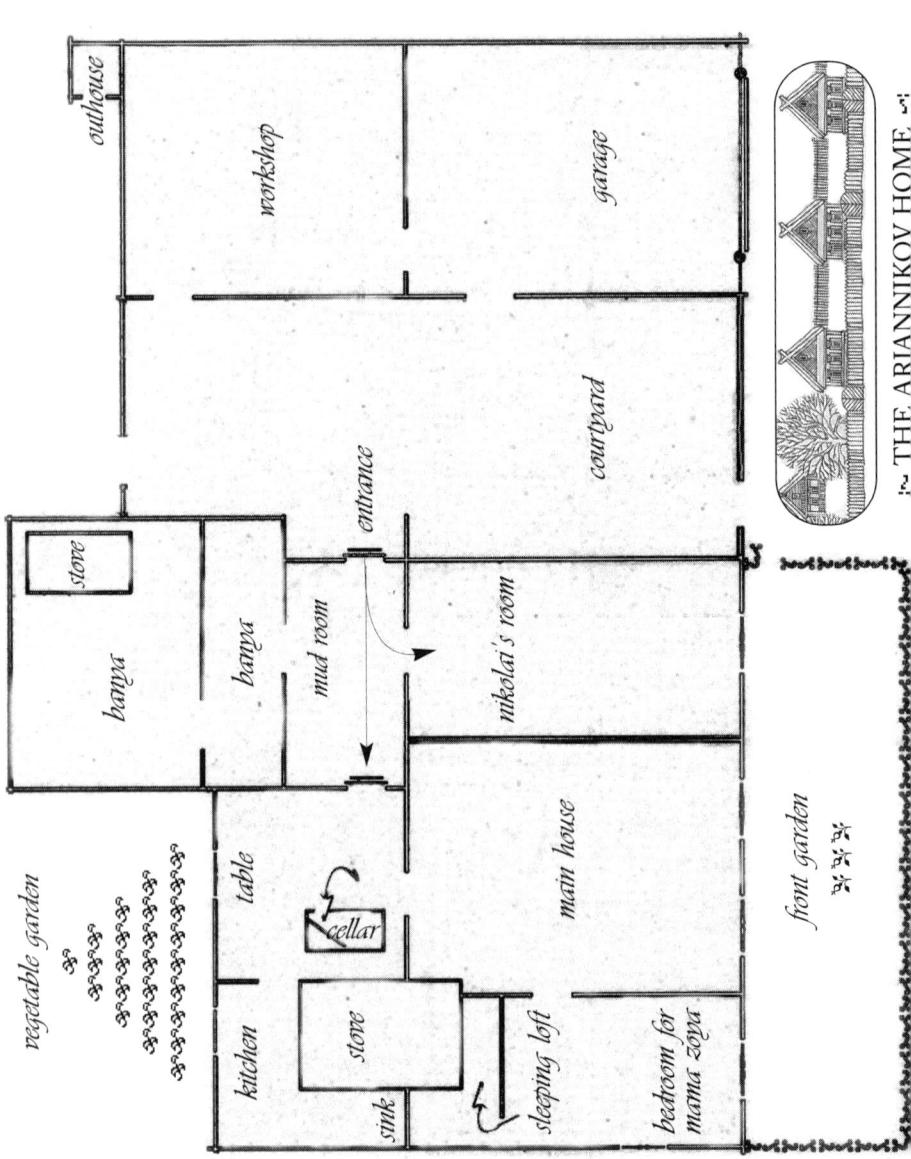

clothes cabinet, and a large hutch that holds Mama Zoya's best plates and tea cups. In the lower right cupboard is a glass bowl filled with individually wrapped chocolates. The wrappers have little pictures of famous places around the world, with lively short word descriptions meant for reading to one another.

People never knock or wait for the door to be opened. It simply flies open and whoever is there blows in with a smile and the breeze and sits down at the kitchen table for a cup of tea. There is no such thing as too many guests.

Anatoly had shown up one day toward the end of our stay with a special invitation to *etee nah rebalky* (or go on a fishing trip) the Saturday before we were to head back to Moscow. The eager look on his face had caused me to say "yes" when Nikolai indicated that the decision was up to me. It was only after Anatoly left that I confessed that I hadn't *completely* understood what he had asked. What were we going to do?

Anatoly and his fellow fishermen headed out at daybreak, while Nikolai and I waited until closer to noon. In the meantime, waiting for the temperature to rise and the sun to come out, we sat at the table in his room cleaning a Soviet era telephone with vodka. (Both the vodka and the effort were because the phone was going to be a gift.)

We had no sooner finished when the door flew open and in blew Lena. Lena lived next door and had known Nikolai since the day she was born. Nikolai leaped up to greet her and promptly invited her to join us. Her gentle laugh filled the room. "Why didn't you ever invite me when we were kids?" She laughed again, saying she'd (still) have to ask her father's permission. Would we wait? She returned in a few minutes wearing a beautiful long coat, a tight close-fitting hat, and a beaming smile.

"Father said yes, but only if we aren't long."

We were headed for Lake Chusovstroya which meant a forty minute drive over beautiful wintery back roads: narrow, winding, and tree lined. The forest was like none I had seen, filled with silver fir trees, as well as pine and birch. This was the woods of Russian novels, thick and untouched, the snow deep, soft, and pure.

We had been descending a gentle grade that would have gone unnoticed had we not come upon a car trying unsuccessfully to get back up from the lake. We stopped to help. The lake was now visible through the trees. The sun had temporarily broken through and sparkled invitingly on the ice. Soon the aged blue Lada was on its way.

With an ancient walkie-talkie we were to let Anatoly know when we arrived. The static alone announced the fact. *Xkkhhhh...* "Allo?" *Xkkhhhh...* "Allo? Allo? Eooo! Anatoly?" Nikolai switched it off. "I think he knows it's us." Within minutes Anatoly's Lada could be seen in the distance flying across the ice. He stopped within a few feet of the shore, shouting directions to help Nikolai navigate the labyrinth of ice ruts.

Soon we were racing side-by-side across the ice until the shore had become no more than a dark line between the lake and the sky. Scattered groups of cars, fishermen, and motorcycles with side seats began to appear ahead of us and, at last, Anatoly's car began to slow to join them. The first one we spotted—with his huge smile, and little pile of fat three inch fish—was Lünchik.

Leonid had inherited the name Lünchik in first grade and never lost it—having never grown much past grade school height. Yet, no one ever made fun of him. "It was impossible," all his friends readily explained. "He was too nice! He cared about everyone. We all wanted him for a friend." Now Lünchik was waving eagerly for us to come join him.

A red auger was produced, with which Lena drilled through two of the three foot thick ice. The hole was then

finished off by Anatoly who promptly plunked down a little canvas stool and invited me to have a seat. As if under the control of a mesmerist, my head snapped down prepossessed by a six inch hole in the ice. Anatoly put the rod, as best he could, in my thickly mittened hand, and then told me to concentrate. After four and a half minutes Lena took a turn. She, too, quickly became disenchanted with life *nah rebalky*, and set the pole down. No sooner had it touched the ground, when Lünchik leaped forward and grabbed it shouting excitedly, *"Ai! Ai! Aiii! Uspek! Uspek!"* Success! Success! Up came a pale, fat, and truly pathetic three inch fish—wriggling.

Typically, Lünchik gave Lena all the credit. Catch in hand, Nikolai, Lena, and I bid the devoted good-bye and headed back, this time finding a spot much farther along the shore in a sunny cove that, it appeared, was free of at least *major* ice ruts. Instead, the shore was a quagmire of thick black mud. Nikolai stepped on the gas, sliding and fishtailing into the depths of it, and heading straight for the woods beyond. Without letting up, we sped across the top of the snow and on toward the road, heading now for a snowbank. If we cleared the bank, the last maneuver would be a 90° turn to get on to the road itself. Before we knew it, we were on the road—and stuck in the opposite snowbank.

In Russia, you must remember, that it is never a question of whether you will get out of a snowbank, but only a question of when. Thus, it was a pleasant surprise to hear help arriving within *minutes*. The sound was still far-off, but clearly approaching and, when it did, it proved to be a motorcycle and sidecar carrying no less than seven jolly Russian fishermen—stacked like precarious potato sacks one on top of another.

For some reason it was agreed that Lena and I should start to walk, leaving the fishermen to figure out how to get the car out. We set off reluctantly, but soon Lena was replacing our uneasiness with colorful childhood stories. Still, with every passing mile, one of us would just casually glance back, thinking we had heard something. The stories would temporarily come to a halt. We'd stop and listen, and then continue on, Lena stoically launching into another episode. At last we were certain we heard men singing and, sure enough, the tittering seven-tiered chorus soon appeared, the ear flaps of their fur hats flapping, and their fists flung flat to their chests as we shouted our thanks. We both breathed a sigh of relief and kept walking. It would be only minutes now. Lena resumed her story with renewed enthusiasm. . . .

When, after another thirty minutes, neither Nikolai nor anyone else appeared, I was no longer listening and

Lena was no longer concentrating. Where was Nikolai?

Just then a huge construction truck appeared from the opposite direction. The good news was, that the truck would certainly be able to get Nikolai out if he was stuck again. The road, however, was too narrow for the truck to pass Nikolai and get down to the lake where it could turn around. The only way out would be to back up. "Ah, that poor truck driver!" I thought to myself. "He has no idea what's waiting for him."

It was, in fact, more than fifteen cars piled up behind ours, none of which could get up the hill. With each new car that appeared, the motorcycle brigade had become more and more discouraged, and finally gave up, saying that they would send help. Enter, the huge green truck.

When it passed us, without a word we turned on our heels and followed it. As it turned out, we had walked a long way. The truck quickly disappeared far beyond our sight. Forty minutes later, Nikolai finally appeared—the car weaving precariously from one side of the road to the other. We quickly turned back, running toward a little rise behind us, urging Nikolai on. Just then, I happened to glance across the road at Lena. The scene was something from *Dr. Zhivago*. Lena, in her long coat and dress, her tall boots and beautiful Russian hat, stood in the deep, Siberian snow-covered woods, out of breath—and anxiously looking into the distance. The only thing missing was the wolves.

Nikolai made the rise and came to a halt a few feet past us. We climbed in and gasped. Nikolai, worn out, and as anxious about us as we had been about him, had not even noticed. Our poor little fat fish was still where he had been left lying on the floor, wrapped in newspaper, next to the heater. It seemed best not to comment that the car smelled as if we were transporting a six foot carp.

Lena's father was not happy when, at last, we arrived home. Nor was our little fish who, to our horror, was alive. We found the large widemouthed jar that only the night before had held pickles, and hastily filled it with water.

The next day Lena came to say good-bye and thank us for taking her along. Father, she said laughingly, was no longer angry, and she, and her husband Yury, had let the little fish go in the river. No, they said, unfortunately they couldn't stay for breakfast. With platter in hand,

Mama Zoya rushed from the kitchen, exclaiming, "Oh, but you must! Anatoly has shared all his fish with us!"

The fish turned out to be a lot for Nikolai Mikhailovich to eat single-handedly.

Meetings and partings

The night before we left there had been a steady stream of friends. They were perched everywhere—in the front room and the kitchen, as well as in Nikolai's room. They brought that joy and laughter that is expressly meant to keep you on your way. Vladimir, Nadershda, and Anatoly (whom you've already met) were in Nikolai's room, along with Nikolai, Feodr, Lutsia, Irina, and Olga, and Olga's nine-year-old daughter Natasha. I was in the front room with Svetlana, and a special family who had become very close to Nikolai. It isn't necessary for you to know the people to imagine the warm, crowded, dimly lit rooms. The table is heavy with food; tea cups clatter, someone bursts into song, another toasts life, another thinks of the parting.

This gathering, like so many others I had experienced in Russia, felt as if someone apart from any one present had given us all an unquestionable gift. It was more than any one person's affection or warmth. It was something higher. Something much more than human affection had allowed us to transcend our greatly different backgrounds and cultures. I'd learned long ago that human affection, on its own, is too easily shaken—and inevitably collapses under the weight of human differences and difficult histories.* It was, however, in moments like these gather-

*Tolstoy wrote in War and Peace, "It is possible to love someone dear to you with human love, but an enemy can be loved only with divine love."

[70]

ings, as if love had all along been trying to show us that there is much more to see about one another than race and nationality. There was our actual spiritual nature, or individuality, that simply called itself *love*. This higher nature allowed genuine closeness—for the simple reason it was, by its very nature, untouched by material histories and human differences.

Lutsia, Irina, and Olga were all close friends. Olga had managed to get us tickets one night to see a performance of *The Marriage of Figaro*. It was the seventieth anniversary of the town's theater. The brilliant production had been sold out—with easily a quarter of the seats being filled with children who laughed and clapped all the way through.

Irina had asked if I'd be willing to teach a university class at the Language Institute. The students, quite fluent in English, were confident, eager to test an American with political and intellectual questions—and somewhat surprised by the answers. "We were certain you would try to sell us on the superiority of America," they had openly challenged. "We were amazed when you didn't!"

I could only assume that they were even more surprised over our decision to decline their invitation to meet with them again.

The students' aims were not unlike those that characterized students here in the 90s, the only difference being that these students were after a fast track Russian version of capitalism. Their defensiveness was not because they were opposed to capitalism, only to the American version of it. There was something sobering, as a result, about the discussion.

After more than ten years, Russians have little feel for democracy—or find it hard to know if it is no more than capitalism. When communism fell, it triggered a moral race much like that between Aesop's proverbial tortoise and hare, the hare being western capitalism, and the tortoise, democracy, *and still at the starting gate*. What could be said to these students thinking only in terms of competing capitalisms—unaware that democracy was even in the race? My thoughts that day went far beyond the small crowded Russian classroom to the other side of the ocean. It was *there*, in America, I suddenly realized, that the race was far from over.

My friendship with Nikolai had begun over a conversation about democracy three years before. He had been one of the organizers of the democracy movement in St. Petersburg during the late 1980s. From one who had narrowly escaped prison (as a result of his involvement), his words compelled respect:

"We thought the West would give us democracy," he had said quietly and matter-of-factly. "Instead, the West gave us capitalism. There is a huge difference between the two in terms of what Russia's future will be. In 1991 the great need in Russia was for ideas, not money."

As a result, the hole made in a fence by a gardener in an old New England Shaker village riveted his attention. It was, Nikolai would say, the most powerful symbol he had seen so far of *democracy* in America. The power of it, was that he understood that it had been an unconscious decision. It was done *naturally* by a simple gardener simply responding to *life itself*. The ability to make such a decision, in Nikolai's mind, was the secret of democracy and freedom. "Everything we do is the result of what we think. One person can build a fence and his thought is to divide people. As soon as I saw the caretaker's fence, I loved the caretaker's life." The instant appreciation of the fence was a way of thinking typical of Nikolai and his friends—as well as most all my Russian friends, and was what had always endeared them to me. Their ideas were ever surprising, ever thought provoking—and inevitably transcended the ordinary, making you feel as if you were no longer breathing smog, but fresh mountain air.

In 1996 Nikolai and several of his friends had established a charter called *The European-Asiatic Peace Initiative* whose stated purpose was "to strengthen friendship between peoples, trust between cultures, and love toward all the nations of the world."

A beautiful site had been chosen at the historic border where Europe meets Asia to build a church—in the sense of a sanctuary or place of refuge. The idea was simply for people of every background and culture to build a refuge in the very place where so many cultures had for so long met and clashed. It was based on the conviction that it is possible for people to think differently—even if that meant thinking the exact opposite of what they thought they had thought before.

Nikolai told me a story once of standing at gunpoint before a soldier who was threatening to kill him. "I hear your words, but they're not what you're thinking," Nikolai had said to the soldier. "Your commander told you to say those words, but you don't really believe them. You have nothing against me, nor I you—and you know it."

Nikolai took me to see the wooded church site. He and his friends had done much research before choosing it. It sat above the main road, impossible to miss. That was the point. The idea of peace was obvious every time you were given a chance to see it. It wasn't necessary to convince anyone that peace made more sense than war—you simply had to continue to put the idea before people as what they already believed. The church would have no preachers or sermons. It would stand as a place, and as an *idea*, and attract people by its sheer rightness.

Such were Nikolai's friends who had come to bid us farewell our last night in the Urals. He and I took turns going back and forth between the rooms, keeping everyone company and tea cups filled. At one point Nikolai came to get me saying, "Someone has come especially to see you!" Surprised, I got up and went toward the door. The first thing I saw was his smile. He wore a thick navy blue knitted cap pulled down to his eyebrows, leaving only his cold red cheeks and huge warm smile visible.

Zhenya was at the door.

To my shock, however, his grandmother was waiting in the courtyard. I hurriedly slipped on a coat and boots and ran to ask her why she was waiting outside! She said they had not wanted to impose with all Nikolai's friends there. I begged them to come in and get warm, even for just five minutes—at least long enough to get something hot for Zhenya to drink. The night was bitterly cold and the wind howling. To no avail, however, could I get them to come in. Zhenya said there was no need, he had only come to say good-bye, and tell me how much he loved his book. He took his grandmother's hand, waved one last time, and then headed out again over the ice and snow— a mile and a half walk home.

The twelfth note card

It was still dark when we left. Unlike Nikolai, I had not managed to "gently go". Zoya Fedorovna did far better, calling out her newly learned American phrase, as the car pulled away, "Aye-Bye, Zhenne! Aye-Bye!" I didn't have the heart to correct her. She was trying so hard. "Aye-Bye, Mama Zoya," I replied teary eyed. "Aye-Bye..."

You can drive for hours across Siberia seeing nothing but vast, endless, stretches of land, tied together with nothing but narrow ribbons of birch trees. We flew over the lonely road partly because the enormity of the scene compels you to do so, and partly because we had a twenty-five hour drive ahead of us. We, meaning Nikolai, Anatoly, and I, had decided to take the southern route as the roads hopefully would be in better condition than the northern ones. Nonetheless, we had two spare tires, about twenty feet of heavy rope, jumper cables, water for the radiator, and enough money to buy me a train ticket back to Moscow should something *really* go wrong. I shared the back seat with numerous bulky cloth sacks filled with homemade bread, bananas, hard-boiled eggs, salted fish, chunks of beef, and apricot *piroschki*.

The road carried us from the stillness of the morning into the brightness of another day, and finally toward the loneliness of night. We'd covered so much ground that we decided, despite our ample stock of food, to stop around 5:00 o'clock at a roadside café to rest and get something hot to eat. It was a luxury, nonetheless. Night loomed before us. We needed to cover as many miles as possible before the roads would once again lie in darkness, and we would be devoid of ready help.

By eight that evening, we had made it to the town of Samara where we needed to cross the Volga River to head north toward Moscow. We slowed down at the sight of a large white road sign. The bridge, it said, was closed. The next crossing was *five hours* out of our way, on a path that, like a large horseshoe, would lead us first to the north, then west, and finally south again, before hooking back up to the main road. Trying to cheer us, Anatoly announced, while bent intently over the map, that we would at least "get to see" Leninogorsk—the birthplace of Lenin.

The car plunged through the darkness over miles of endless road. The later it got, the more the temperature dropped until, close to midnight, we were in the middle of a snowstorm that turned the road to black ice. Without warning, the car spun once, twice, three times, and came to a halt, at last, in a ditch. We climbed out in the silence, each unconsciously drawing on hidden reserves of strength. Our flashlight bleakly revealed that our car was not in a good position. Yet, less than five minutes in this desolate place, the truly miraculous happened: the blackness of the night was pierced by the headlights of a truck which stopped to help. Nikolai lay on his back on the wet cold ground working to get our rope fastened to the car. The truckdriver meanwhile fastened his line and told me to cross the road in case the car lunged forward out of control. The gears of the truck could be heard shifting into place. The truck inched forward, the lines became taunt, groaned under the strain . . . and then broke. The truckdriver was shaking his head anxiously, watching in silence as Nikolai barely got the lines retied.

The process was repeated twice more before we were out, but for Nikolai and Anatoly the worst was not over. We climbed back into the car and only managed to inch our way along. Both men were exhausted and these were now the hardest hours, between midnight and dawn. For the first time on the trip I heard Nikolai quietly say that he was nervous. It was only after we were safely back in Moscow that I asked him why. He explained that if our car hadn't been able to traverse the icy roads there would have been no way out. We would have had to simply wait for the weather to change and the road to clear—be that a day, or a week. Knowing that in two days my visa would expire and I must catch a plane flight home, he was praying that there'd at least be a way to send me on alone. He had resolved in his mind that if another truck passed us, he would ask the driver to get me to a train station. As it turned out, we didn't pass another car or truck for several hours. By then our car had gained momentum and, after two more hours, we had driven out of the storm.

Now the gas tank was low. We reached a station, and a rather young boy, maybe fifteen or sixteen, came out to pump the gas, despite the fact that it was around 3:00 in the morning. As always, I heard Anatoly double check our directions. But this time I heard a reply that I knew I'd never forget. The boy said, "I'm sorry, I don't know the way. I've never been down that road before." It struck me the moment it was said as describing Russia itself on its long, difficult road from communism to democracy. It was then, that I suddenly realized that this journey had taken me a long way down a road of understanding. And to Nikolai *that*, and not miles, had always been the real distance that stood between the United States and Russia.

The bright sun glared on the Moscow skyline as we merged on to the "Golden Ring," the six-lane highway that surrounds the city. It was noon—thirty hours after we'd left the Urals. Within twenty-four more I was on my way back to America. In the weeks ahead I would begin to pick out a few little things to send to Nikolai and each of the friends who'd so willingly helped us. Since I knew they would open their gifts together, I intended to simply include one long letter to all of them in the package. At the last minute, however, I decided to ask a close friend, Valerie Christle, if I could get a dozen or so different note cards from her with photographs of our area. That meant, however, delaying the box several days while I wrote each person a note. Twelve notes in Russian was a considerable task. Knowing that Nikolai would be in the Urals only long enough to build the banya for his mother, if I delayed too long the box might not make it while he was there. A Russian, I knew, would risk it and so I did.

Nikolai called everyone the day the package arrived. They came that night and had *shashlik* (in the courtyard) and opened their gifts. Mama Zoya got out the bowl of chocolates and then, one by one, they began to open their cards and read them. It was then that they discovered the hole in the fence. It was quite amazing when you thought about it. One day a gardener needed no more reason than joy to put a hole in a fence, on another, someone thought to take a photograph, and then a postman did his best to deliver his packages on time—and all the while, none of them knew what they were accomplishing.

How differently, it seems, we all would live, if we resolved never to forget that what we do makes a difference.

Long ago a kindly people
BUILT THE CANTERBURY SHAKER VILLAGE. THE YEARS WENT ON & A DAY CAME TO BE WHEN A BROTHER THOUGHT TO BUILD A GRANITE & PICKET FENCE AROUND THE MEETING HOUSE. MANY MORE YEARS CAME AND WENT & ANOTHER BROTHER ADDED TO THE FIRST BROTHER'S HANDIWORK A GROVE OF YOUNG HYDRANGEAS. FOR REASONS UNKNOWN THE FENCE WAS FINALLY TAKEN DOWN AND THE BUSHES LEFT TO GROW FREELY & TO THEIR GLORY. LONG YEARS AFTER THE KINDLY PEOPLE CEASED TO BE, THE VILLAGE CARETAKERS REBUILT THE FENCE AND HEEDED A YOUNG GARDENER'S REQUEST TO TAKE CARE TO MAKE A HOLE IN IT.

MAKE A HOLE IN THE FENCE

Thanks to many people,
SINCE JANUARY 2001 NEARLY 2100 LIBRARY
AND CHILDREN'S GIFT BOOKS HAVE BEEN
BOUGHT, MORE THAN 400 LETTERS SENT
BETWEEN RUSSIA & THE U.S., & OVER 300
PHONE CALLS MADE. BY THANKSGIVING, A
SISTER-LIBRARY PROJECT WILL HAVE BEEN
LAUNCHED BETWEEN THE TOWNS OF
WAKEFIELD NEW HAMPSHIRE AND
PROHAROVKA RUSSIA.

AFTERWORD:
A BOOK THAT BECAME A LIBRARY

Gilman's Corner

THE REVIVING OF ONE small library in a remote Russian village, the full effect of which none of those who made it possible would ever know, but nonetheless chose to do, all began with something equally unlikely: a children's book published by an unknown publisher.

In the spring of 1999 we began work on an anthology of international children's stories whose sole purpose was to give children the opportunity to discover the very best of their world. In addition, if we could get people to buy the book, the proceeds were to be used to buy new books for rural Russian villages.

We'd just begun work on the book, when I got a call one day from someone I didn't know. "This is Priscilla Harper," the woman began. "You gave a talk not too long ago and mentioned that you were publishing an anthology of international children's stories. I'd like to ask you about it."

I instantly regretted mentioning it in the talk, for the simple reason I was now faced with having to confess to the woman that the book had only one story at that point. To my amazement, that didn't bother her in the least.

What mattered most to her was that such a book was in the making. She'd wait. Her little daughter was only four. An hour later, she called back with the names, phone numbers, and addresses of people in over a dozen different countries. Over the next two years, I would be in awe of the contacts Priscilla would make effortlessly with people I would never have had the courage to approach.

One of her dear friends in Scotland, for instance, had told her about Duncan Williamson. He was the son of *travellers*, or Scottish gypsies, famed for their storytelling despite the fact that traveller children, when Duncan was growing up, rarely received more than a grade school education. Yet, from his father's stories, Duncan, the seventh of sixteen children, not only grew up feeling genuinely loved, but received "something that was going to stand us through our entire life".

Priscilla got hold of one of his books, fell in love with it, and promptly sent me his address. He was well-known and enormously talented. "How could he possibly have time for an utterly unknown publisher who can't pay him either a cent or a shilling?" I argued with her.

Priscilla persisted. *"Just write and ask!"* I did, but the letter was returned unopened. Duncan had moved and so, with relief, I called Priscilla to say that was that. An hour later she called me back. "I have his new address."

In the intervening hour, she had called the Postmaster of Strathmiglo Scotland, explaining the entire project, as well as our dilemma. The Postmaster was glad to be of help. He would find the address and ring her right back. Priscilla then explained that she was calling from America.

"Never you mind lassie. Jus' give me yur number and I'll ring you back." Thus another letter was sent off which Duncan answered immediately. "You can use as many stories as you want from my Books as the copy Rites all Belong to me and you have my Permission to use as many stories as you want and no one can stop you as long as I say you can use my stories. Please keep in touch and I will send you on another Book you can use." Every book he sent included a sprig of heather.

Priscilla would also make a truly miraculous contact with Sue Hendrickson, paleontologist and discoverer of *Tyrannosaurus Sue*. Sue would write an incredibly encouraging story about her discovery, in large part because she was already involved in getting books into children's hands in Guatemala and was eager to support all such efforts.

Another friend of Priscilla's, a Peace Corps worker in West Africa, Molly Lipscomb, would hike out into the wilderness, tape recorder in hand, to capture a wonderful story from Khady Diop, a Mauritanian grandmother, and brilliant storyteller.

Another trek would be made by a journalist for *The Christian Science Monitor*, Robert Marquand, who would win the heart and help of India's Ruskin Bond. Mr. Bond allowed us to use his internationally acclaimed story *The Blue Umbrella*.

In every case the authors helped us wholeheartedly. Rachel Crandel, a teacher, author, and growing expert on

South America, gave us two stories from that part of the world, as well as a contact that resulted in the book being reviewed in *Publishers Weekly*. Lise Richardson, a close friend of mine born and raised in Denmark, would put an old edition of Hans Christian Andersen's stories into my hands that included a brilliant and little known work called *The Honest Shilling*. She then introduced me to her friend, author Jasmine Tsang from China, who not only gave us a story, but kindly contacted a close Australian friend of hers who tracked down the young Aboriginal storyteller, Pauline McLeod. China and Australia were thus added to the book, and so it grew step by step.

As stories from country after country began to fall into our laps, we next wondered if we could find an astronaut who would help us, someone who had looked out on our world and would remind us of the wonder of it all. Dr. Rhea Seddon, NASA astronaut, kindly sent a truly touching story that began, "Once upon a space shuttle..."

And so the book was gathered and nurtured by people who fully believed the world still had beautiful stories to tell. The book would open with a moving story from the small, war-torn country of Ingushetia about a grandfather's lesson to his grandson of the worth of peace over "a half-meter of land," and would end with another true story from England called "Rainbows".

A story called *Six Inches to England* became the title of the book. It would make the simple point that there was a time for each of us, as children, when "distance had no meaning—nor foreigners nor strangers."

The book took over two years of patience and persistence. Even more, it took the help of people near and far working together and bound together by "a generosity of spirit". These were individuals who were willing to help people they would never know or meet—but whose well-being nonetheless mattered to them.

Again and again that fact would deeply move Nikolai, and over and over again I would hear him telling people that the library had not been accomplished merely "with money," but with the heartfelt caring of many, many people. Oddly enough, it was not so much the books, but the fact that the project had always been all out of proportion, so to speak, that touched everyone's heart: so much work, for such a long time—for one small Russian village. Why had they "bothered"?

Because such things give the most life. There is no other explanation. It is the smallest act of good that *most defies* the apparent enormity of darkness and evil. We soon would be overwhelmed without these defiant acts of "impossible good". They appear and we breathe again, we laugh again. We're reassured that discouragement was a trick and that there is no reason not to go forward.

To quote Nikolai, "There always will be something to be said for doing those things that 'reason' screams make absolutely no difference. For they are the things, like the hole in the fence, *that give life.*"

JEANNIE FERBER

List of illustrations

i	Canterbury Shaker Village. Photo: Valerie Christle.
iv	Laptee. A gift from Anatoly Portnov. The laptee were made by his father.
vi	Map of journeys where libraries have been done.
viii	Sergei Evegenevich and Olga Anatolevna, directors of Vetoshkino Middle School. Inset: village home.
4	Reshetnikov home. Vetoshkino, Russia.
11	Tatyana Reshetnikov.
19	Mikhail Reshetnikov.
22	Emelia Mikhailovna, director, Votckoya Primary School.
22	Ludmilla Ivanovna and J. Ferber. Votckoya.
23	J. Ferber and Emelia Mikhailovna. Votckoya.
31	Nikolai Arjannikov.
36	Votckoya road. Illustration by Peter Ferber.
38	Nikolai's bedroom window. Pervouralsk, Russia.
44	Vladimir and Nadershda Terehov.
52	Sunflower seed packet. Price: five kopecks. Sovietskoya.
56	Zoya Fedorovna Arjannikov. Inset: Aunty Zoya and Mama Zoya.
61	Nikolai Arjannikov.
62	Arjannikov home. Pervouralsk, Russia.
65	Lena Sukhorukova, ice fishing.
66	Leonid Kondrashin, ice fishing.
69	Anatoly Portnov and prize fish.
80	Letter from Tatyana Reshetnikov, Vetoshkino.
81	Emelia Mikhailovna, director, Votckoya Primary School.
88	Lake Chusovstroya: Leonid, Nikolai, Anatoly, Lena.

NIKOLAI MIKHAILOVICH ARJANNIKOV

Arjannikov was born and raised amongst the gentle people of the Ural Mountains. He studied law in Leningrad, but soon would spend some ten years in war zones searching for, and finding ways to convince others of, "the science of how not to kill".

He returned to Leningrad and found himself in the forefront of the democracy movement of the late 1980s and early 1990s that eventually led to the break up of the Soviet Union.

He would stand atop the tanks with Yeltsin and at his side the day Yeltsin became President of the Russian Federation. Arjannikov served one term in the Duma, or Parliament. He has an honorary doctorate degree from Campbell University in North Carolina in recognition of the role he played in the democracy movement.

His most passionate goal remains to build a church, or place of refuge, at the border of Europe and Asia where all peoples may meet "to learn war no more".